BELOVED

FRANCIS CHAN
WITH MERCY GORDON

150 YEARS STRONG
DAVID C COOK

BELOVED
Published by David C Cook
4050 Lee Vance Drive
Colorado Springs, CO 80918 U.S.A.

Integrity Music Limited, a Division of David C Cook
Brighton, East Sussex BN1 2RE, England

DAVID C COOK®, the graphic circle C logo and related marks
are registered trademarks of David C Cook.

Library of Congress Control Number 2025938238
ISBN 978-0-8307-8905-4
eISBN 978-0-8307-8096-1

© 2025 Crazy Love Ministries

The Team: Michael Covington, Stephanie Bennett, Gina
Pottenger, Dana Carrington, Susan Murdock
Cover Design: Will Cotterall
Photography: James Wong
Illustrations: Eliana Chan
Cover Image: "Christ and St. John," by Ary Scheffer (1795-1858)

Printed in the United States of America
First Edition 2025

1 2 3 4 5 6 7 8 9 10

060525

At David C Cook, we equip the local church around the corner and around
the globe to make disciples. Come see how we are working together.

Discover more. Be the difference.

Visit **DavidCCook.org/Donate**

To everyone who has prayed for me to experience breakthrough in receiving God's love, thank you. I really believe God heard and answered, and this book is a testament to that.

CONTENTS

INTRODUCTION

In heaven, God sits on a throne, beaming with glory far beyond anything you've ever seen. The thunderous sound of millions of angels worshipping Him is like nothing you've ever heard. If I could approach our holy God right now and ask Him how He feels about you, what do you think He would say?

Actually answer that.

Your answer reveals a lot about what you believe about God and yourself.

It affects everything that matters.

"Peter turned and saw the disciple whom Jesus loved..." (John 21:20).

Five times in his gospel, John refers to himself as "the disciple whom Jesus loved." Throughout history, John has been remembered as the beloved disciple.

If this was your last day on earth, how would you be remembered?

How would you like to be remembered?

Again, how you answer those questions will tell you a lot about yourself, so actually answer them. For most of my life, I wanted to be known for my integrity, sacrificial love, or powerful teaching. I admired the stories of Elijah calling down fire, Peter walking on water, and Paul suffering greatly to spread the gospel.

I could not relate in the same way with John. The idea of simply being identified as God's beloved never crossed my mind. I considered it my purpose in life to be useful, not to be loved. But over time, I've learned that you can live a seemingly useful life that is void of the very thing you were created for: the enjoyment of God. You serve Him but don't enjoy Him. What's worse is that you're not sure if He enjoys you.

Only recently did I realize the word "beloved" is two words combined: be loved. It hit me because it conveys the idea that being someone's beloved is completely passive. I'm not good at passive. Many of us are terrible at receiving, but that needs to change. We are God's beloved children, and He wants us to be able to simply *be* loved. Not striving, just believing and enjoying and resting in His perfect love. Like John resting his head on Jesus' chest (John 13:23–25).

The Problem We Face

When's the last time you sat in silence, doing absolutely nothing productive, and just enjoyed God's presence? When's the last time you truly believed, deep in your bones, that God was smiling at you—not because you did something impressive, but simply because you're His?

My friend was with his wife in the Amazon, staring at an untouched area of the rainforest. It was wild, lush, and overflowing with beauty: orchids, bananas, cacao. As they looked at the cacao tree, he commented, "Imagine the amount of cocoa beans that tree has produced over decades, only for them to fall to the ground." His wife had a different reaction that had nothing to do with production and harvesting: "I think God must just enjoy the beauty of His creation; to see the flowers flourish and fade, to see the fruits ripen and then fall. He made it, and it's enough that He takes pleasure in it."

For many of us, our minds are obsessed with production. It carries over into our relationship with God. We try to accomplish as much as possible in order to please Him. What began as a joy starts to feel like a burden or obligation. We serve until we're exhausted, hoping God notices our efforts. We battle doubts about our salvation and constantly wonder if we're doing enough. It's hard to imagine a God who enjoys watching us, like a parent who sneaks into his toddler's room just to watch her sleep.

I know because I've been there.

On my fiftieth birthday, I gathered my family and friends to pray for me. I had recently read 1 John 4:18b, "Whoever fears has not been perfected in love." I knew it described me, but I didn't want to believe it. It felt shameful to admit that I was only ninety percent sure of my salvation.

Is it okay for a pastor to tell his church that he still fears God's rejection?

Wouldn't that have a detrimental effect on their faith?

I started a church and saw it grow to thousands of people. I wrote books that were read by millions of people. I founded a Bible college, planted churches, preached to masses but still battled insecurity. Insecurity probably motivated most of my actions. Maybe it stemmed from never being loved by my dad, or maybe it's from my Bible college days when I was taught to constantly evaluate myself and others. Whatever the origin, it needed to stop. I didn't want to live another day without the perfect love that casts out all fear.

By the grace of God, He brought me to the point where I wanted freedom more than a reputation. I wanted to be perfected in love more than I wanted to be admired. I chose to be honest with myself and those I loved.

The good news is that God heard my prayers and those of my friends. He opened my eyes to lies that I had believed and continues to teach me how to enjoy Him daily. In short, He rescued me and wants to do the same for you. I think that's why you're holding this book.

I have a conviction and a belief that God gave me for this book that is simple but life-changing: abiding in the love of God frees us from all insecurity and leads us into a lifetime of joyful, worshipful obedience.

Read that again.

I used to think that God created me to impact the world. I now think God created me to have another person to lavish His grace upon. He didn't create Adam and Eve because He needed gardeners. He abounds in love, so He created beings to receive it.

This isn't about trying harder. It's about believing deeper. It's not about doing more for God; it's about receiving more from God. It's about moving from performance-based religion to love-based relationship.

When you read the passage below, I hope you can see the heart of a loving Father.

> So we have come to know and to believe the love that God has for us. God is love, and whoever abides in love abides in God, and God abides in him. By this is love perfected with us, so that we may have confidence for the day of judgment, because as he is so also are we in this world. There is no fear in love, but perfect love casts out fear. For fear has to do with punishment, and whoever fears has not been perfected in love. We love because he first loved us. (1 John 4:16–19)

Did you catch that? "We love because he first loved us." Not "we love in order to earn His love" or "we love hoping one day He'll love us back." His love comes first. It's the foundation, not the reward.

The Invitation

This book is for those whose Christian experience feels contractual rather than romantic. For those who deep down believe that God is disappointed in them. For those who serve out of obligation rather than overflow.

It's for those who have a hard time believing that a holy God pines for them. It is far easier for you to declare your love for Jesus than to boast in His love for you. You fight against sin and serve sacrificially, but it's driven by insecurity instead of the overflow of love.

My prayer is that God's love is not wasted on us. That He doesn't stand with open arms as we serve frantically in disbelief. May we break the enemy's lies and just receive. Just be loved.

In the coming chapters, I want to walk alongside you as we rediscover what it means to be loved by God—not as a theological concept, but as a daily reality that transforms everything about how we live. I want to help you see that God's greatest desire isn't your service or sacrifice—it's your heart. He wants you to know, beyond any shadow of doubt, that you are deeply, completely, eternally loved.

And from that place of security—of being loved—will flow the kind of obedience that doesn't exhaust you but exhilarates you. The kind of service that doesn't drain you but delights you. The kind of sacrifice that feels less like duty and more like privilege.

That's the Christianity we were meant to live. That's the freedom Christ died to give us.

Be loved, beloved.

1.

CHAPTER ONE

INSECURITY

N ot everyone who says to me, 'Lord, Lord,' will enter the kingdom of heaven, but the one who does the will of my Father who is in heaven. On that day many will say to me, 'Lord, Lord, did we not prophesy in your name, and cast out demons in your name, and do many mighty works in your name?' And then will I declare to them, 'I never knew you; depart from me, you workers of lawlessness.' (Matthew 7:21–23)

The worst thing that could ever happen to a human being is to hear God say "depart from me." When you read those words of Jesus, have you ever had even the slightest fear that you might be one of the "many" who will be rejected? After all, this is terrifying. This is eternal! Passages like this motivate some of us toward action. We try to sin less, give more, pray more, serve more. We want to prove to God and to ourselves that we are one of the real disciples. Yet the harder we try, the more elusive that security becomes.

The Problem of Doubt

A friend of mine recently discovered a growth on her thyroid gland and was told a biopsy was necessary. "But don't worry," the doctor said. "There's only a ten percent chance that it's cancer." Isn't it interesting that even though it's ninety percent not cancer, just that ten percent makes us feel uneasy until the biopsy comes back completely negative?

Let me ask you something pretty directly: If you were to die today, are you sure you would go to heaven? How sure?

> Seventy percent?
> Eighty percent?
> Ninety percent?

And is that enough for you? We're not talking about a medical test result here. We're talking about the difference between experiencing the wrath of God for our sins eternally or experiencing perfect peace, joy, love, and pleasure forever. I am willing to bet that the majority of you reading this book, if you are brutally honest, have doubts about your salvation. You've never voiced the concern because that kind of doubt is unacceptable in Christian circles.

At several events I spoke at recently, I asked people to raise their hands if they sometimes doubted their salvation. It broke my heart to watch hand after hand go up. As a father, I can't imagine how horrible it would feel if my kids were only eighty percent sure that I loved them. How much more must it grieve God to see His beloved children insecure in their relationship with Him?

My Own Journey with Doubt

I wasn't always insecure. As a high school student, I was secure in what Christ did for me. I was thrilled to be a Christian and confident of my future with Jesus. I didn't analyze my faith to death; I just enjoyed it.

Insecurity really started to take root in me during my Bible college days. In my theology classes I was introduced to the concept of lordship salvation. In short, it's the truth that a person cannot have Jesus as their Savior without having Him as Lord. It is an important truth in a world where people want a savior but not a king.

In a society that rebels against all forms of authority, Christians are clamoring for a Savior that we don't have to follow. But the Scriptures cannot be any more clear: He is Lord. In fact, salvation is predicated on us declaring Him as Lord (Romans 10:9–10). Like the old song goes, "He is Lord, He is Lord! He is risen from the dead and He is Lord! Ev'ry knee shall bow, ev'ry tongue confess that Jesus Christ is Lord."

It's nonsensical to think that Jesus can be just Savior and not Lord. It's as ridiculous as saying "I want Francis to be my friend, but I want him to stop being Chinese." Jesus Christ is the King of the universe. He is the Creator and Judge. He is Lord. He doesn't lessen who He is in order to enter into a relationship with you. He's the same yesterday, today, and forever.

The problem was not in the doctrine of lordship but in how it played out in many of our lives. Our school kept asking us to examine ourselves to see if Jesus truly was the Lord of our lives. Again, this isn't necessarily bad. After all, Paul tells the Corinthians, "Examine yourselves, to see whether you are in the faith. Test yourselves. Or do you not realize this about yourselves, that Jesus Christ is in you?—unless indeed you fail to meet the test!" (2 Corinthians 13:5).

I specifically remember having a discussion with some of my friends in our dorm. We were questioning our devotion to God when one of the girls said, "Can we really ever know if we have made Jesus Lord of our lives? Don't you think it's something we won't know for sure until we die?" Several of us kind of nodded our heads. After all, God is the only one who can judge whether or not we treated Him as Lord. I look back now and think, what a horrible conclusion! So now we spend the rest of our lives wondering whether or not we have surrendered everything, thus making Him Lord. Since our salvation depends on this, we are actually doubting our salvation. It's just like Satan to rob a bunch of Bible college students of their joy in God's grace by plaguing them with insecurity.

We spent so much time questioning our love for Christ that we rarely took time to stare at His love for us! Yet that is the foundation of our faith! Our love is a love of response. We love because He first loved us. It's the enjoyment of Christ's love that leads us to love Him in return. It's His love that makes us want His lordship.

The Free Gift of Lordship

Can Jesus be my Savior without being my Master? That people even ask this question shows the real problem. We see His authority as a bad thing. We love the thought of Jesus paying the price for our sins, but we dread the thought of Him controlling our lives.

The lordship of Jesus is supposed to be a gift! He is willing to be your King. You are welcomed into His kingdom where He rules. Throughout history, believers have seen His commands to be a blessing, leading us to life.

> For what great nation is there that has
> a god so near to it as the LORD our God
> is to us, whenever we call upon him?
> And what great nation is there, that
> has statutes and rules so righteous as
> all this law that I set before you today?
> (Deuteronomy 4:7–8)

Moses reminded the people how blessed they were to have God near them, giving them His wonderful rules. Read Psalm 119 some time. Does this sound like someone who dreads the thought of God's lordship and rules?

> Deal bountifully with your servant,
> that I may live and keep your word.
> Open my eyes, that I may behold
> wondrous things out of your law.
> I am a sojourner on the earth;
> hide not your commandments from me!
> My soul is consumed with longing
> for your rules at all times. (Psalm 119:17–20)

We've all given in to sin. We have tasted the pleasure of it and struggled with the temporary enjoyment and lasting regret. The lack of lasting satisfaction may have led you to chase greater highs and deeper perversions that ultimately end in death (see James 1:14–15). Hopefully now you have accepted the reality that you cannot find satisfying pleasure on your own. Jesus offers to save you from futility as well as the penalty for your disobedience. He offers a way of life that leads to life everlasting and inexhaustible.

> You make known to me the path of life;
> in your presence there is fullness of joy;
> at your right hand are pleasures
> forevermore. (Psalm 16:11)

You were on a futile path that ends in death. He offers to take you down a different path that leads to life. He will give you the directions and the power to follow. He's willing to do it all for free! Far from being a burden, His lordship is meant to be a gift! He offers to inhabit you and lead you to "fullness of joy" and "pleasures forevermore." Lordship was not meant to be a goal where you tirelessly strive to make Him Lord. It is a free gift where the Lord enters you and mysteriously leads you to life by making you love His ways.

What shall we say then? Are we to continue in sin that grace may abound? By no means! How can we who died to sin still live in it? (Romans 6:1–2)

What then? Are we to sin because we are not under law but under grace? By no means! (verse 15)

... having been set free from sin, have become slaves of righteousness. (verse 18)

Other Roots of Insecurity

While my personal struggle with insecurity was largely rooted in this doctrinal tension, there are many reasons insecurity is so pervasive among believers. As I've had the opportunity to preach and minister in places all over the world, here are some of the most common roots of doubting God's love for us that I've come across.

Past Experience

Even if you believe that God loves you as a Father, that concept may be completely foreign to you if you did not grow up in the security of a loving home.

Growing up, I had virtually no relationship with my dad. My mom died giving birth to me, so my dad tried to give me up for adoption. My aunt intervened and I was sent to Hong Kong to live with my grandmother instead until she could no longer care for me. When I was five, my dad was forced to take me back. He didn't want me, and he never spoke to me except to criticize or punish me.

I do remember one moment of affection when I was eight years old: he put his arm around me for about thirty seconds while we were on our way to my stepmother's funeral. Besides that, the only physical touch I experienced were the beatings I received when I disobeyed or bothered him.

Our earthly relationships affect our view of God. As I look back on my early life, I can see how my upbringing contributed to decades of struggling to grasp the love of God. However, as I reflect on my life now, I am overwhelmed by the grace of God. Though I never received the love of a father, He allowed me to taste it from being on the other side. As a father, I got to experience a father's love by giving it.

Lisa and I have seven kids and five grandchildren, and we're all crazy about each other. I remember on our anniversary a few years back, Lisa looked at me and said, "Do you think there's anyone happier than us?" We seriously couldn't imagine there being a happier couple. Our lives are so full and rich. We love God and experience His love more every year, and now we get to watch our kids and grandkids fall in love with Him. It is truly abundantly more than anything I could have asked or imagined.

I say all of this because I know that many of you reading this have baggage from your past that hinders your relationship with God. But I also know and have experienced that He is a Redeemer, a Healer, and a Restorer of our broken lives. Your story will look different from mine, but your restoration will be just as complete. He knows each of our hurts and brings healing to each of us uniquely.

Continual Sin

Sometimes we don't feel the joy of salvation because of an ongoing struggle with sin. We don't feel comfortable laying our heads on the chest of our Judge. That's not always a bad thing. There are times when you should feel deeply disturbed. This is a gift from God. The enemy would want you to think this uneasy feeling is because God doesn't love you, when it's actually the opposite.

And have you forgotten the exhortation that addresses you as sons?

"My son, do not regard lightly the discipline of the Lord, nor be weary when reproved by him. For the Lord disciplines the one he loves, and chastises every son whom he receives."

It is for discipline that you have to endure. God is treating you as sons. For what son is there whom his father does not discipline? If you are left without discipline, in which all have participated, then you are illegitimate children and not sons. Besides this, we have had earthly fathers who disciplined us and we respected them. Shall we not much more be subject to the Father of spirits and live? For they disciplined us for a short time as it seemed best to them, but he disciplines us for our good, that we may share his holiness. For the moment all discipline seems painful rather than pleasant, but later it yields the peaceful fruit of righteousness to those who have been trained by it. (Hebrews 12:5–11)

If you are sick to your stomach because you're in sin, praise Him! Far from being a sign that He no longer loves you, it's proof that He does. Rather than becoming defensive or defeated, recognize that God is lovingly correcting you because He wants you to share in His holiness.

I've gone through seasons in my life where I felt distant from God, only to realize that He hadn't moved—I had. My sin was creating the separation, not His lack of love. And that conviction was actually His kindness pulling me back.

Cynicism

There are some people who always tend to gravitate toward the negative. Perhaps it's a sort of defense mechanism. If you always expect the worst, you won't be surprised or hurt when it happens. Or maybe pessimism is what was modeled for you by parents or other authority figures who struggled with bitterness.

Cynical people tend to fixate on wrongs that have been done to them and allow the resulting mistrust and skepticism to color their outlook on life. When you hear that God is rich in mercy, abounding in steadfast love and faithfulness, it sounds too good to be true. We have to be careful though. There is a point when our cynicism becomes offensive to God: when it causes us to doubt His promises.

> May the God of hope fill you with all joy and peace in believing, so that by the power of the Holy Spirit you may abound in hope. (Romans 15:13)

Pause right now and ask the Holy Spirit to make you a person of hope. You can't be cynical **and** *"abound in hope."* You can't be filled *"with all joy and peace"* if you keep replaying past offenses or hurts in your mind. You can't be filled with both cynicism and the Holy Spirit. You have to choose. The almighty Holy Spirit longs to heal you of unbelief and fill you with perfect peace. We don't have to beg Him to change us. We just have to surrender to the changes He wants to make. Pray that He would begin that work right now.

God Wants You Secure

Whatever the reason may be, there is great news for those wrestling with doubt.

> So we have come to know and to believe the love that God has for us. God is love,

and whoever abides in love abides in
God, and God abides in him. By this is
love perfected with us, so that we may
have confidence for the day of judgment,
because as he is so also are we in this
world. There is no fear in love, but perfect
love casts out fear. For fear has to do with
punishment, and whoever fears has not
been perfected in love. (1 John 4:16–18)

Celebrate as you read those three verses. I'm bursting
with gratitude when I think of this being God's heart for
me. Don't just read and analyze it. Try to picture it. Picture
yourself perfectly abiding in God, in perfect love, with
perfect confidence. Judgment is coming, but fear is the last
thing on your mind. You abide in God's perfect love.

Picture yourself like a toddler cuddling in the arms of a
perfectly loving father, completely protected from any
possible harm. This is God's desire for you.

Good Fear, Bad Fear

As we think about perfect love casting out all fear, it's
important to acknowledge that the Bible also commands
us to fear God and speaks of the fear of God as a blessing:

It is the LORD your God you shall fear.
Him you shall serve and by his name
you shall swear. (Deuteronomy 6:13)

The fear of the LORD is the beginning of
wisdom, and the knowledge of the Holy
One is insight. (Proverbs 9:10)

The friendship of the LORD is for those
who fear him, and he makes known to
them his covenant. (Psalm 25:14)

For as high as the heavens are above
the earth, so great is his steadfast
love toward those who fear him.
(Psalm 103:11)

So what does a healthy fear of God look like? I want to be careful not to overdefine things because I believe there is some mystery around this topic. But I do want to point out two common misconceptions that lead many astray.

The first is to conflate the fear of God with the fear of condemnation. This results in an underlying insecurity that sucks the joy and freedom out of the Christian life. Pick up your Bible right now and read Matthew 10:28–31.

Meditate on it before the Lord. Ask the Spirit to show you how you are supposed to simultaneously "fear him" and "fear not."

The second is to throw off the fear of God along with the fear of condemnation. This is what can happen when we rely on our own logic to define who God is. If God is love, then He can't possibly be terrifying, right? If God is rich in mercy, surely there isn't such a thing as an eternal hell.

This results in a shallow understanding of the love of God and can lead to a sense of entitlement toward the grace of God rather than humble gratitude and wonder. Hear Paul's warning to the Gentiles regarding entitlement:

> So do not become proud, but fear. For if God did not spare the natural branches, neither will he spare you. Note then the kindness and the severity of God: severity toward those who have fallen, but God's kindness to you, provided you continue in his kindness. Otherwise you too will be cut off. (Romans 11:20b–22)

This verse, and many of the verses that talk about the fear of God, can come across as harsh. If God really desires intimacy with us, why would He want us to fear Him? In Jeremiah 32, God explains why:

> And they shall be my people, and I will be their God. I will give them one heart and one way, that they may fear me forever, for their own good and the good of their children after them. I will make with them an everlasting covenant, that I will not turn away from doing good to them. And I will put the fear of me in their hearts, that they may not turn from me. I will rejoice in doing them good, and I will plant them in this land in faithfulness, with all my heart and all my soul. (Jeremiah 32:38–41)

The fear of God allows us to continue in God's kindness, which is His desire for every person that He has made. It guards us from the pride and sin that crouches at the door, ready to separate us from God. So the fear of God is not at odds with the love of God. Rather, it is the refuge from which we can freely enjoy the love of God.

> In the fear of the LORD one has strong confidence, and his children will have

> a refuge. The fear of the LORD is a
> fountain of life, that one may turn away
> from the snares of death. (Proverbs
> 14:26–27)

I can't help but fear God. To know Him is to fear Him. Even the demons shudder. Is it possible for a human being to know of God's glory without fearing Him? Even righteous Job and John, the beloved disciple, were terrified when they "saw" Him (see Job 42:5; Matthew 17:6). Fear isn't something we need to work at. It is the natural result of believing in the nature of God. If I'm surfing and see the fin of a great white, I don't need to muster up fear. Or if I'm hiking and encounter a mountain lion, I make no effort at fearing it.

The sight of a Being so powerful causes instant fear, but knowing that He loves us with an everlasting love should make us the most fearless people on the earth!

> When then shall we say to these things?
> **If God is for us, who can be against
> us?** He who did not spare his own Son
> but gave him up for us all, how will he
> not also with him graciously give us all

things? Who shall bring any charge against God's elect? It is God who justifies. Who is to condemn? Christ Jesus is the one who died—more than that, who was raised—who is at the right hand of God, who indeed is interceding for us. Who shall separate us from the love of Christ? Shall tribulation, or distress, or persecution, or famine, or nakedness, or danger, or sword? As it is written,

"For your sake we are being killed all the day long; we are regarded as sheep to be slaughtered."

No, in all these things we are more than conquerors through him who loved us. For I am sure that neither death nor life, nor angels nor rulers, nor things present nor things to come, nor powers, nor height nor depth, nor anything else in all creation, will be able to separate us from the love of God in Christ Jesus our Lord. (Romans 8:31–39)

There's a danger in writing a prayer at the end of a chapter. Most readers will see it as cute and mildly creative. That's the last thing I want. Don't treat this as the bow on a package. It's more like the plug for your toaster. Enthusiastically come before His throne of grace right now and pray this simple prayer:

> "God, lead me into the perfect love that removes all fear of judgment. Lead me into the godly fear that takes me into deeper friendship with you."

II.

CHAPTER TWO

REVELATION

Many are oblivious to the spiritual battle that rages on around us. I Peter 5:8 says, "Be sober-minded; be watchful. Your adversary the devil prowls around like a roaring lion, seeking someone to devour." Imagine if you looked up from this book to see a lion slowly circling you, getting ready to pounce. What would you do? Run? Scream? Pray? Whatever your reaction might be, I seriously doubt it would be to pick this book back up and continue reading like nothing was happening. And yet, that is exactly the kind of casual attitude we can have toward Satan and the demonic forces.

For much of my life, I didn't think or talk much about the demonic realm because I didn't want to be one of "those people" who see demons in everything. But the Bible is very clear that evil forces exist, and that their goal is to steal, kill, and destroy our faith.

> For we do not wrestle against flesh and blood, but against the rulers, against the authorities, against the cosmic powers

over this present darkness, against the
spiritual forces of evil in the heavenly
places. (Ephesians 6:12)

I believe that one of the greatest schemes of the enemy is
to keep us insecure. Think about it—if someone is totally
secure in the perfect love of an almighty God, they become
fearless. The opinions of others don't sway them. The
coming judgment day doesn't scare them. But when the
enemy gets even the slightest foothold of doubt regarding
those truths, he uses it to cripple us, often to devastating
effect. This isn't just what Satan does; it's who he is.

Thief, Accuser, Deceiver, Murderer
Thief

> The thief comes only to steal and kill and
> destroy. I came that they may have life
> and have it abundantly. (John 10:10)

Satan steals joy. If you're not happy in Jesus, Satan
is winning, because joyless Christianity is powerless
Christianity. Even the demons *believe* in God, so Satan
knows that he doesn't necessarily have to attack your
belief in God's existence. He just needs to impair your
relationship with God. That is where the power and
beauty of the Christian life lies.

Satan will try to get you to think about anything other than the grace of God. He will keep you fixated on your circumstances or suffering. He will entice you with distractions and temptations. He will tell you that you don't have time to gaze at God's beauty. You have too many things to do and problems to fix.

Accuser

> And I heard a loud voice in heaven, saying,
> "Now the salvation and the power and the
> kingdom of our God and the authority of his
> Christ have come, for the accuser of our brothers
> has been thrown down, who accuses them day
> and night before our God." (Revelation 12:10)

Satan heaps guilt and shame. He makes you think you're still dirty rather than having been cleansed of all unrighteousness. He will make you dwell on the ugliness of your past rather than your present beauty and future glory.

Deceiver

> He was a murderer from the beginning,
> and does not stand in the truth, because
> there is no truth in him. When he lies, he
> speaks out of his own character, for he is
> a liar and the father of lies. (John 8:44)

Satan will do anything he can to keep our hearts and minds from the truth that sets us free. Oftentimes it is more subtle than outright contradiction. He distorts the love and grace of God. He gets you questioning if you've done enough to deserve the grace of God or whether you've sinned too much to attain it. During the temptation of Jesus in Luke 4, Satan even tries to use Scripture to deceive Jesus.

> And he took him to Jerusalem and set him on the pinnacle of the temple and said to him, "If you are the Son of God, throw yourself down from here, for it is written,
>
> 'He will command his angels concerning you, to guard you,'
>
> and
>
> 'On their hands they will bear you up, lest you strike your foot against a stone.'"
>
> And Jesus answered him, "It is said, 'You shall not put the Lord your God to the test.'" (Luke 4:9–12)

The enemy wants you to believe (consciously or subconsciously) that your insecurity is biblical. He will isolate passages in your mind like "You therefore must be perfect, as your heavenly Father is perfect" (Matthew 5:48) from passages like "For by grace you have been saved through faith. And this is not your own doing; it is the gift of God, not a result of works, so that no one may boast," (Ephesians 2:8–9) to keep you fixated on yourself and your sin rather than the saving work of Christ. He wants to blur the line between salvation and sanctification so that any time you mess up, it sends you spiraling into doubt instead of running to the throne of grace.

Murderer

> *We should not be like Cain, who was of the evil*
> *one and murdered his brother. And why did*
> *he murder him? Because his own deeds were*
> *evil and his brother's righteous. (1 John 3:12)*

Abel did nothing to Cain, and yet Cain murdered him. Why? Because he was "of the evil one," and the evil one hates when God's children are in perfect relationship with Him. I have felt the strongest attacks in decades while writing this book. The enemy wants to murder my childlike joy before it spreads to others. As Satan used Abel's brother to murder him, he will use anyone to try to kill our joy and security!

Weapons of Our Warfare

Our enemy is very real, and I believe he is more active than any of us truly realize. We have to start recognizing that our doubt and insecurity are not random, they're demonic. And we need to take up the weapons that have been given to us to fight this spiritual battle.

> For though we walk in the flesh, we are not waging war according to the flesh. For the weapons of our warfare are not of the flesh but have divine power to destroy strongholds. We destroy arguments and every lofty opinion raised against the knowledge of God, and take every thought captive to obey Christ. (2 Corinthians 10:3–5)

The Word

One of our greatest weapons in this struggle is the Word of God. This is why biblical literacy is so important. We need to know the full counsel of God and develop our powers of discernment so we're not blown and tossed by Satan's deceptions, however subtle they may be. But we don't just need to know the Word comprehensively; we need to know it intimately. This is where meditation is so helpful and important. While there are some seasons where I focus on covering the full breadth of Scripture, there are others where I focus on a single passage or verse for days.

Which is the greatest command?

There are 31,102 verses in the Bible. We don't have time to meditate on every verse. Which ones will you choose? Every preacher disproportionately refers to certain passages, and every denomination emphasizes certain topics and verses. This has a massive impact on those who listen. Who decided that we should memorize John 3:16 rather than John 3:36? My point is that there are many factors that cause us to focus on certain portions of Scripture. While Isaiah 66:2 teaches us to "tremble" at His words, I noticed my tendency to tremble at His commands but not His promises. I spent many years overcorrecting those who preached about His grace, mercy, and love. I witnessed so much apathy, immorality, and an overall low view of God in the church. I made it my quest to bring balance to the church culture. I would preach about His holiness, wrath, judgment, and hatred of sin. In my mind, people were skirting these topics, so I would emphasize them. Was it wrong to do so? Maybe. I guess we'll find out in the end.

What I do know is that there is a form of heresy in preaching certain attributes of God to the neglect of others. I also know that I rarely, if ever, meditated on the following verses to my detriment. You may be the type that meditates on these verses to the neglect of others. This book was written primarily to those who tend to focus on their own failures rather than His mercy, grace, and love. Please take these next pages more seriously than any other part of this book. Actually meditate and enjoy. Spend ten minutes rejoicing over each verse. Put aside your hurriedness and your felt need to accomplish a task. Your King says that only one thing is necessary. Sit at His feet. Gaze at His beauty. Enjoy Him.

MEDITATE

Sit at His feet. Gaze at His Beauty. Enjoy Him.

You shall not bow down to them or serve them, for I the LORD your God am a jealous God, visiting the iniquity of the fathers on the children to the third and the fourth generation of those who hate me, but showing steadfast love to thousands of those who love me and keep my commandments.

~ Exodus 20:5–6

I have loved you with an everlasting love; therefore I have continued my faithfulness to you.

~ Jeremiah 31:3b

But you, O Lord, are a God merciful and gracious,
   slow to anger and abounding in steadfast love and faithfulness.

~ Psalm 86:15

Have mercy on me, O God, according to your steadfast love; according to your abundant mercy blot out my transgressions.

~ Psalm 51:1

"For the mountains may depart and the hills be removed, but my steadfast love shall not depart from you, and my covenant of peace shall not be removed," says the LORD, who has compassion on you.

~ Isaiah 54:10

There is no fear in love, but perfect love casts out fear. For fear has to do with punishment, and whoever fears has not been perfected in love.

~ 1 John 4:18

For as high as the heavens are above the earth,
   so great is his steadfast love toward those who fear him;
as far as the east is from the west,
   so far does he remove our transgressions from us.
As a father shows compassion to his children,
   so the LORD shows compassion to those who fear him.

~ Psalm 103:11–13

But the steadfast love of the LORD is
from everlasting to everlasting
on those who fear him,
  and his righteousness
to children's children,
to those who keep his covenant
  and remember to do his
commandments.
~ Psalm 103:17–18

To him who loves us and has freed
us from our sins by his blood....
~ Revelation 1:5b

They refused to obey and were not
mindful of the wonders that you
performed among them, but they
stiffened their neck and appointed a
leader to return to their slavery in
Egypt. But you are a God ready to
forgive, gracious and merciful, slow
to anger and abounding in steadfast
love, and did not forsake them.
~ Nehemiah 9:17

I have been crucified with Christ.
It is no longer I who live, but Christ
who lives in me. And the life I now
live in the flesh I live by faith in the
Son of God, who loved me and gave
himself for me.
~ Galatians 2:20

For God so loved the world, that he
gave his only Son, that whoever
believes in him should not perish
but have eternal life.
~ John 3:16

Know therefore that the LORD your
God is God, the faithful God who
keeps covenant and steadfast love
with those who love him and keep
his commandments, to a thousand
generations.
~ Deuteronomy 7:9

May the Lord direct your hearts
to the love of God and to the stead-
fastness of Christ.
~ 2 Thessalonians 3:5

But God shows his love for us in
that while we were still sinners,
Christ died for us.
~ Romans 5:8

See what kind of love the Father
has given to us, that we should be
called children of God; and so we
are.
~ 1 John 3:1

The LORD your God is in your
midst, a mighty one who will save;
he will rejoice over you with
gladness; he will quiet you by his
love; he will exult over you with
loud singing.

~ *Zephaniah 3:17*

Put on then, as God's chosen ones,
holy and beloved, compassionate
hearts, kindness, humility, meek-
ness, and patience, bearing with
one another and, if one has a com-
plaint against another, forgiving
each other; as the Lord has forgiven
you, so you also must forgive. And
above all these put on love, which
binds everything together in perfect
harmony.

~ *Colossians 3:12–14*

Greater love has no one than this,
that someone lay down his life for
his friends.

~ *John 15:13*

But God, being rich in mercy,
because of the great love with
which he loved us, even when we
were dead in our trespasses, made
us alive together with Christ—by
grace you have been saved....

~ *Ephesians 2:4–5*

In this the love of God was made
manifest among us, that God sent
his only Son into the world, so that
we might live through him. In this
is love, not that we have loved God
but that he loved us and sent his
Son to be the propitiation for our
sins. Beloved, if God so loved us, we
also ought to love one another.

~ *1 John 4:9–11*

"Yet even now," declares the LORD,
"return to me with all your heart,
with fasting, with weeping, and
with mourning; and rend your
hearts and not your garments."
Return to the LORD your God, for
he is gracious and merciful, slow to
anger, and abounding in steadfast
love; and he relents over disaster.

~ *Joel 2:12–13*

No, in all these things we are more
than conquerors through him who
loved us. For I am sure that neither
death nor life, nor angels nor rulers,
nor things present nor things to
come, nor powers, nor height nor
depth, nor anything else in all
creation, will be able to separate us
from the love of God in Christ Jesus
our Lord.

~ *Romans 8:37–39*

But this I call to mind, and therefore I have hope: The steadfast love of the LORD never ceases; his mercies never come to an end; they are new every morning; great is your faithfulness. "The LORD is my portion," says my soul, "therefore I will hope in him." The LORD is good to those who wait for him, to the soul who seeks him. It is good that one should wait quietly for the salvation of the LORD."

~ Lamentations 3:21–26

I will sing of the steadfast love of the Lord, forever;
   with my mouth I will make known your faithfulness to all generations.
For I said, "Steadfast love will be built up forever;
   in the heavens you will establish your faithfulness.

~ Psalm 89:1-2

Keep yourselves in the love of God, waiting for the mercy of our Lord Jesus Christ that leads to eternal life.

~ Jude 21

Prayer

The other weapon that I want to focus on is prayer. A few years ago, I prayed a simple prayer that I now pray regularly: "Lord, show me where I am deceived." We can all look back at life and recall instances when we were tricked. We believed something that we now know is a lie. As they say, hindsight is 20/20. But are you deceived right now? The correct answer is "I don't know." Anyone who answers, "No, I am not currently being deceived," does not understand the definition of the word.

Because I have been praying that prayer regularly, God keeps exposing my blind spots. I have been loving it. Every correction has made my life happier and more peaceful. Honestly, I was expecting the process to be more grueling and painful, but even that expectation reveals something about me. At the time, I had no idea that God was going to show me that I don't enjoy Him as much as He wants.

While God has worked powerfully through my personal prayers, I need my friends to fast and pray for me too. It absolutely makes a difference. The enemy is always whispering or screaming lies in my ear. I can honestly say that I want to enjoy God's love more than anything, but the enemy keeps trying to drag me into doubt. This is why when people ask me how they can pray for me, I usually respond with this prayer from Ephesians 3:

> For this reason I bow my knees before the Father, from whom every family in heaven and on earth is named, that according to the riches of his glory he may grant you to be strengthened with power through his Spirit in your inner being, so that Christ may dwell in your hearts through faith—that you, being rooted and grounded in love, may have strength to comprehend with all the saints what is the breadth and length and height and depth, and to know the love of Christ that surpasses knowledge, that you may be filled with all the fullness of God.
>
> Now to him who is able to do far more abundantly than all that we ask or think, according to the power at work within us, to him be glory in the church and in Christ Jesus throughout all generations, forever and ever. Amen. (verses 14–21)

I share this because I think many of us are hesitant to be honest about our struggles out of fear that it might mean we don't truly know Jesus or that other people will perceive it that way. But this, too, is demonic. Scripture tells us:

> Therefore, confess your sins to one another and pray for one another, that you may be healed. The prayer of a righteous person has great power as it is working. Elijah was a man with a nature like ours, and he prayed fervently that it might not rain, and for three years and six months it did not rain on the earth. (James 5:16–17)

> But if we walk in the light, as he is in the light, we have fellowship with one another, and the blood of Jesus his Son cleanses us from all sin. If we say we have no sin, we deceive ourselves, and the truth is not in us. If we confess our sins, he is faithful and just to forgive us our sins and to cleanse us from all unrighteousness. (1 John 1:7–9)

Our prayers for one another are powerful and effective. Our confession opens the door for healing. If you find yourself hitting a wall trying to believe that God really loves you as passionately and steadfastly as He promises in all those verses you just meditated on, I strongly encourage you to share that with believers in your life and ask them to pray for you.

Supernatural

Ultimately, the insecurity that cripples so many of us is not something that is going to be solved by reading a book. It is a spiritual issue that requires a supernatural solution. There is mystery to it. This is why Paul writes that "God's love has been poured into our hearts through the Holy Spirit who has been given to us" (Romans 5:5b).

So often, especially in the West, we focus chiefly on the intellect. And it is good to study and know truth. But the reality is, many of us know all the right answers about the love of God but struggle to experience it in our hearts. I have a dear friend who went to seminary with me. He told me recently about how miserable he was for fifteen years following our seminary experience. He kept thinking there would be a point where he produced enough fruit to rest in Christ, but the harder he strove, the more impossible it felt.

When he finally understood that Romans 5:5 is a subjective truth (more than an objective truth, but something he was supposed to experience), he began praying over and over that the Holy Spirit would pour God's love directly into his heart. He prayed this for five years! Then it happened. He recounts how he was working out in a weight room when the Spirit revealed the Father's love to him. He describes it as "heaven on earth." He spent the next five hours sobbing over the love of God. Today, if you meet him, you know you're with a person who deeply enjoys the love of God. Spiritual understanding is not merely the product of effort. We need the Holy Spirit to pour God's love directly into our hearts and silence the voice of the accuser.

How badly do you want to experience this? Do you have a desperation in you that burns like a fire? Your whole being screams, "I must have this! I want this more than anything! If I can only have one thing granted, I must know the love of God!" I have met too many people who threw up a quick prayer and concluded, "It didn't happen for me." This shows that they don't understand the value of this treasure. My friend prayed desperately for five years before all the ingrained legalism finally broke and the love of God flooded his soul. I'm not saying it always takes this long, but it speaks to his diligence and desire. When you spend more time praying for a girlfriend, husband, child, healing, or anything more than you pray to know the love of Christ, it reveals something. You undervalue the treasure of knowing the love of Christ.

III.

CHAPTER THREE

IDENTITY

And behold, a voice from heaven said, "This is my beloved Son, with whom I am well pleased." (Matthew 3:17)

This is the statement that God makes at Jesus' baptism and again during the transfiguration. He could have said, "This is my all-powerful Son," or "This is my perfect Son," but He didn't. The one thing that the Father wanted everyone to know was that Jesus was His beloved! If God were to introduce you to the world, would He use the same sentence? John would say yes.

I used to think it was strange that John calls himself the disciple whom Jesus loved. It would be like one of my kids saying, "I'm the beloved child." It sounds inappropriate, not to mention arrogant! But the truth is, John's statement is perfectly appropriate. John understood the depths of God's love for him—that he could take on the identity of the beloved along with *Jesus Himself*! And suddenly everything else seemed utterly insignificant in comparison.

This is the logical response to such a radical truth. We are the strange ones who want to be known for anything else.

I still remember entering a new school in third grade. A kid I befriended started telling me about the other kids. That's David—he's a great athlete. That's Alisa—she's crazy smart. That's Benny—he's the fastest kid in the school. That's Cindy—she's the hot girl, obviously. I was the new kid who eventually became known as the Chinese kid (there weren't many of us). From an early age, we are labeled. Most of us don't like the labels we were given, so we fight to shed those and be known for something better. Usually, however, the new labels aren't much better, nor do they satisfy. The doctor, the fitness instructor, the lawyer, the millionaire, the influencer...

John escaped that entire circus altogether. We are often identified by what we are obsessed with, and for this reason John became known as the beloved. John's writings show that he was fascinated by loving statements that came out of the mouth of Jesus. He remembered them and wrote them down. Let's not forget that John was the one who recorded John 3:16—the most famous verse on earth. He's also the one who recorded this statement that some of us have a hard time believing: "As the Father has loved me, so have I loved you" (John 15:9).

John actually heard Jesus say this to him, and he trusted that Jesus meant what He said. When he called himself the beloved disciple, it was not wishful thinking. It was because he heard the words of Jesus and believed them. It had nothing to do with arrogance, and everything to do with faith. John was expressing faith in Christ's love, not his own lovability.

False Gospel #1: Jesus as the Means to an End

When I became a Christian, I was immediately taught—though not in these exact words—that Jesus was the means to an end. "Pray this prayer, and you won't go to hell." Later it evolved into, "Follow Jesus, and your life will be blessed." Or "Trust God, and He'll fix your marriage." While there's some truth to these statements, do you see the fundamental problem? That's not the gospel.

The good news of the gospel of Jesus Christ is not that if you follow Him everything will go well for you, you'll get whatever you pray for, and everything in your life will work. The good news of the gospel is that if you follow Jesus, you get ... that's right ... Jesus! You get Him and He is more than enough for you no matter what your circumstances are.

It is true that He saves us from hell and God can help your marriage and family, but it's a problem when we emphasize Jesus being the pathway to these treasures. It's idolatry, not the gospel, when we elevate gifts above the Giver and sell Jesus as a means to get the things we want more than Jesus Himself. People lose sight of the fact that God *is* the treasure!

> The kingdom of heaven is like treasure hidden in a field, which a man found and covered up. Then in his joy he goes and sells all that he has and buys that field. (Matthew 13:44)

I am convinced that most "Christians" in America view Jesus as a means to an end. This is why they question His goodness or even His existence when they don't receive what they expected from Him. This is largely due to the way we have marketed Christianity to them. We have not emphasized the great treasure! It's as though we don't think He's enough. We need to sweeten the deal by throwing in a stable income or a wife or a child. When Paul talks about how we have been blessed, he says, "Blessed be the God and Father of our Lord Jesus Christ, who has blessed us in Christ with every spiritual blessing in the heavenly places, even as he chose us in him before the foundation of the world, that we should be holy and blameless before him. In love he predestined us for adoption to himself as sons through Jesus Christ, according to the purpose of his will, to the praise of his glorious grace, with which he has blessed us in the Beloved" (Ephesians 1:3–6).

In 2009 I bought a salvaged Toyota Corolla from a friend of mine for a great price. It had hardly any miles on it, and I thought I'd have it forever, but in 2016 I gave the keys to my new son-in-law Justin along with my daughter Rachel—it was a package deal. When I walked Rachel up the aisle at their wedding, I bawled my eyes out. I was flooded with memory after memory of twenty-one years of life with this girl that I love with all my heart. When we got to the end of the aisle, we hugged for a really long time. I just didn't want to let go.

Imagine if, at that moment, Justin looked at me and said, "Man, thanks for the Toyota."

Are you kidding me? I'm giving you my beloved daughter, and all you're thinking about is the car? That would be so outrageous and offensive, but that's what the church in America sounds like today.

I think about the depth of what I felt in that moment for my daughter, who had been in my life for twenty-one years, and then try to imagine what God feels for His beloved Son who has been in perfect relationship with Him for all of eternity. It's unfathomable, and yet that's what God has blessed us with. We are blessed in the Beloved. Not only that, He has adopted us to Himself as sons and daughters. We can now take on the identity of God's beloved along with Jesus Himself! Praise His glorious grace! Repent of any times that you have coveted lesser blessings. What more could we possibly ask for?

False Gospel #2: Works as the Means to Jesus

Perhaps you know that Jesus is the treasure, but you are caught in a cycle of trying to work your way into His love. This too is a false gospel. The reality is, in any relationship, love is not something that's earned; it's something that's received. And yet, many of us find ourselves constantly striving to earn the love of God and the people around us. Why is that?

Many of us have spent a great portion of our lives working to gain the approval of others. Whether it's a parent, teacher, or boss, we have learned that right actions receive approval. I get good grades, I receive praise from my parents. I work efficiently, I get a raise.

This can cause us to confuse approval, which is something you earn, with love, which can't be earned. Think about it—the Bible teaches that God loved us even when we were dead in our trespasses and sins. He didn't approve of our actions; in fact, He hated them. But love is who He is, and even when we were His enemies, He loved and desired us enough to die for us.

Some of you were loved from the moment you were conceived. Your parents rejoiced at hearing your heartbeat while still in the womb and couldn't wait to get their first glimpse of your face. You did nothing to earn that. They loved you for nothing you had done, and they continue to love you. Meanwhile, some of you had no one joyfully welcoming you into this world. Like me, you were an inconvenience, being shuffled around until someone finally agreed to take the responsibility of raising you. Your only survival mechanism was to earn favor or approval by right actions. You quickly learned how to earn the approval of others.

It could be that you were never loved, so you are confused in understanding the love of God. It could be that you have been loved but didn't recognize it as such. The point is there are many of us who have been stuck in a cycle of earning approval, and we think we are earning love. We then project that onto our relationship with God. We think He loves us when we act appropriately and withholds His love whenever we fail.

Love is not something we need to work for. When we forget that, we can get overly fixated on our own actions and become either discouraged or prideful. If we're having a bad week, we might start doing things to try to make up for it and prove to God that we're really sorry. If we're having a good week, we might subconsciously pat ourselves on the back for being "good enough." Ultimately, it's a vicious cycle that keeps us focused on self, separating us from God.

The True Gospel

This is the true gospel, the gospel that captivated and transformed John: Jesus is the way, and He is the end!

> For God so loved the world, that he gave his only Son, that whoever believes in him should not perish but have eternal life. (John 3:16)

> And this is eternal life, that they know you, the only true God, and Jesus Christ whom you have sent. (John 17:3)

In Him, we have been given a whole new identity that completely transforms our lives. We are adopted into an eternal family and betrothed in marriage to a perfect bridegroom. I want you to realize that an adoption or a marriage is not just a one-and-done transaction—it's the beginning of a lifetime of loving relationship. To abide in God's love is to live in this new identity and to enjoy it more and more each day.

Beloved Children

Have you ever meditated on the uniqueness of us calling God "Father"? If you've been in church for a while, you might hear Him called Father so much, it can start to feel commonplace. But there's something very special about Jesus saying when you pray, call Him "Our Father" (Matthew 6:9).

In Ephesians, Paul writes, "For this reason I bow my knees before the Father, from whom every family in heaven and on earth is named" (Ephesians 3:14–15).

So the word *Father* means He is our origin. You exist because your heavenly Father decided to create you. You were not an accident. He may have used two human beings on the earth, but He Himself is your Father as in the originator, the creator.

Jeremiah 1:5 is one of my favorite verses: "Before I formed you in the womb I knew you, and before you were born I consecrated you; I appointed you a prophet to the nations."

Think about that for a minute. Before you existed in your mother's womb, God already knew you. It's like we originated with Him in essence first somehow and then were formed in substance in the womb. And before we took a breath, He had already appointed specific things for us to do. We were created, personally and purposefully, by God Almighty. This is what we declare when we call Him our Father, as the psalmist does in Psalm 68:5: "Father of the fatherless and protector of widows is God in his holy habitation."

Some of you probably did not have a great father. Maybe you had an average dad or a terrible relationship with your dad or no relationship with your dad or your dad left the home or maybe you don't even know who your dad is. And so when you hear the word *father* and you try to think of God, all this baggage is with you.

Some of you, on the other hand, have really good fathers, and there's a challenge that comes with that too. You may not feel the need to rely on your heavenly Father in the same way because there isn't the same void in your life. Sometimes I tell my kids that I have no concept of what it would be like to be loved by an earthly father the way they have. And sometimes I feel like they are missing out on that. I almost worry that their affection for me might somehow detract from their affection for Him. There was something nice about transferring all of my thoughts of fatherhood to God. Nothing competes for that position in my life or affection.

Whatever your situation, the enemy will try to use it to rob you of the joy of knowing God as Father. But the truth is "you did not receive the spirit of slavery to fall back into fear, but you have received the Spirit of adoption as sons, by whom we cry, 'Abba! Father!'" (Romans 8:15).

Something mysterious happened when you became a believer where you received the Spirit of adoption, through whom we cry, "Abba!" Paul talks about this again in Galatians 4: "But when the fullness of time had come, God sent forth his Son, born of woman, born under the law, to redeem those who were under the law, so that we might receive adoption as sons. And because you are sons, God has sent the Spirit of his Son into our hearts, crying, 'Abba! Father!' So you are no longer a slave, but a son, and if a son, then an heir through God" (verses 4–7).

In Romans it says we cry out, and here in Galatians it says the Spirit of God in our heart cries out. I don't know exactly what that looks like, but I know it's different from me simply opening my mouth and saying the words, "Abba, Father." Somehow, supernaturally, my spirit and the Spirit of God join together to literally cry out from the core of my being that He is my true Father! My identity is forever changed. I am His beloved child, and no one will snatch me out of His hand!

If you have never literally cried, "Abba! Father!" by the Spirit from the core of your being, do it. Don't look at this passage and assume it's referring to something figurative. Some of us grew up in traditions that made everything seem vague and intangible. There's nothing in these passages that should lead us into thinking this way. Take time now to get alone in a quiet place and cry out to your Father. It is an amazing privilege and one of the most enjoyable things you can do.

Radiant Bride

In Ephesians 5, Paul writes, "Husbands, love your wives, as Christ loved the church and gave himself up for her, that he might sanctify her, having cleansed her by the washing of water with the word, so that he might present the church to himself in splendor, without spot or wrinkle or any such thing, that she might be holy and without blemish" (verses 25–27).

And in Revelation 19:6–8, John writes, "Then I heard what seemed to be the voice of a great multitude, like the roar of many waters and like the sound of mighty peals of thunder, crying out, 'Hallelujah! For the Lord our God the Almighty reigns. Let us rejoice and exult and give him the glory, for the marriage of the Lamb has come, and his Bride has made herself ready; it was granted her to clothe herself with fine linen, bright and pure'—for the fine linen is the righteous deeds of the saints."

Have you ever meditated on or marveled that we are the bride of Christ? We are therefore the recipients of His protection, provision, and affection! I grew up in a church tradition that didn't speak about this much. As a result, I had not thought deeply about this until recently. Being the bride of Christ was a phrase I was familiar with, but it was not a reality I enjoyed. My marriage to Lisa is so real to me. I deeply enjoy it. My marriage to Jesus has felt far less tangible and enjoyable. I'm guessing this is true for many, and this is why we have found our identity in something other than being the beloved bride of Christ.

My favorite part of officiating a wedding is when the bride walks down the aisle. Everyone stands, the music swells, and the bride appears in her dazzling wedding dress. In those moments, I love watching the groom. Sometimes there are tears. Sometimes he's smiling from ear to ear. Sometimes I actually hear an audible gasp because he's stunned by how beautiful she looks. He can't take his eyes off his bride as she walks toward him. Nothing else in the world exists in his eyes but her.

That's when it hits me. That's how Jesus looks at us—at His church. That's what Paul means when he calls us the bride of Christ. Jesus isn't just our Lord, our King, our Savior—He's our Bridegroom who gazes at us with that same intensity of love. The One who trembles with joy over us. The One who sees us walking toward Him, flawed and fumbling as we are, and is absolutely captivated.

I read the Song of Solomon recently. It was the first time I had ever been able to put myself in the story. Believers have historically taken this book to be allegorical, referencing God with Israel or Christ with the church. Over the past century, some have argued against the historical interpretation saying that it is just a book about intimacy between a husband and wife. I believe it can be both. While I have believed it in my mind, this is the first time I have ever been able to personalize it.

In my natural mind, it feels uncomfortable and even blasphemous to think of God longing for me as the book describes. I'm too ugly, dirty, insignificant compared to

Him. How could a holy God have such intense feelings and desire for a weak and sinful human? My rational mind can't make sense of it until I force myself to stop looking at my failures and shortcomings and stare at His love. His love is not like our love. It's holy love. He is holy love.

His holy love is seen in the book of Hosea when Hosea is told to pursue the prostitute Gomer even after she deserts him and has sex with other men. No rational human would marry and love a random prostitute, much less pursue her extravagantly after she deserts him. God's love is not like ours. That's what it means to be holy. He is set apart from us. He is capable of loving in ways we cannot fathom. Keeping this in mind enables us to put ourselves in the Song of Solomon. Pray that He gives you grace to believe in His passionate desire for true intimacy with you. Many of us believe He loves us, but it is still abstract. It doesn't even remotely resemble the passion of a groom for his bride. Pray. We are in process. We see as in a mirror dimly (1 Corinthians 13:12). Pray that God gives you strength to see how wide and long and high and deep....

Heresy with Good Intentions?

One of the elders at our church recently shared with me that he was meditating on Romans 8:1, "There is therefore now no condemnation for those who are in Christ Jesus," but something in him did not want to share this verse with the church. He quickly realized the root of his fear: his reasoning. If he lets people know that they are safe from condemnation, it will result in greater sin. If they are insecure or afraid, this will motivate them to produce the right actions. There was something manipulative in him that wanted to keep the congregation insecure. If the goal is merely avoiding sinful behavior, this works. If the goal is abiding in love, this is a huge stumbling block.

God warns those who cause His children to stumble (see Matthew 18:6). It is no small sin to teach in such a way that it causes God's children to doubt their Father's love. Even now, think about those you influence as well as those who have influenced you. Were you brought up in a system that motivated you to obedience through constant doubting of your salvation? Are you passing that on to your children and disciples? The great news is that you can pray right now to a God who is rich in mercy and full of grace. He will both forgive you and empower you to break the cycle.

John didn't use insecurity to motivate actions. On the contrary, he addresses his disciples as "beloved" ten times in his letters. Those who enjoy the love of God can't help but want their loved ones to enjoy it as well. John wanted us all to take "beloved" as our identity. As we will talk about later in the book, being secure in Christ will actually yield greater results. For now, God wants us to trust and celebrate our new identity!

Let's slowly cherish every word of this verse: "See what kind of love the Father has given to us, that we should be called children of God; and so we are" (1 John 3:1a).

See: The word means to pay special attention to something. Pray that God enlightens you so you can truly know and internalize this truth.

what kind of love: Recognize that God's love is distinct. When He tells you that He loves you, it is set apart from the love humans can give. His love is holy.

the Father: This is His identity! God reveals Himself to us through the perfect Father and Son relationship. Celebrate the fact that our God has been eternally known as Father. Meditate on the implications of that. Cry out to your Abba Father.

has given to us: Love is something the Father has given— not something we need to earn. Open your hands now and receive all that He wants to offer you. Receive adoption, love, protection, and the eternal inheritance He has given to us.

that we should be called children of God: Don't lose your excitement over the fact that you've been given this title. Who are we, mere humans who aren't guaranteed another breath, that we are given this ridiculous privilege? Celebrate this in His presence.

and so we are: This is our identity. This is who we are.

In a world full of people searching for identity, constantly changing how they want to be identified, let's rejoice forever as the bride of Christ and children of the perfect Father.

God longs for us to run to Him with the same abandon as a child who knows they are loved, delights in that love, and never doubts it for a second. Or a bride who basks in being the object of affection of the groom, who loves her so much that he was not just willing to die for her, but joyfully die for her (see Hebrews 12:2).

That's your identity: the beloved of God. Not because of anything you've done, but because of who He is and what He's done for you. This is who you are. And when we truly believe it, it changes everything.

IV.

CHAPTER FOUR

LIFE

I received a voice message twenty-five years ago that I still vividly remember. I was away from the family, speaking in a different state when my daughter Rachel left a message. At first, all I heard was sobbing, then a little five-year-old voice repeatedly cried, "I miss you, Daddy. Please come home!" If I remember correctly, she cried loudly on the message for over a minute—heartbreaking. I called Rachel to remind her that I would be home soon. I assured her that I hated being away from her also. When we got off the phone, she went into my room and grabbed the last shirt I wore. This became her nightly ritual when I was gone. It made her feel close to me.

Rachel's family of five recently moved two thousand miles away from us. Now I'm the one who wants to leave sobbing voicemails for my grandchildren! I hate being so far away from them. Sometimes I walk by their old house and imagine them running up to hug me. Prayers, memories, and phone calls keep me somewhat close, but I'm always plotting to figure out when I can see them again.

Do you see God as a real person, wanting to be with us and creating opportunities to do so? Over and over throughout the whole narrative of the Bible, God shows how much He wants to be near us. He walked in the garden with Adam and Eve, filled the temple with His glory, became flesh and dwelt among us, and gives us this vision of our eternal destiny: "Behold, the dwelling place of God is with man. He will dwell with them, and they will be his people, and God himself will be with them as their God" (Revelation 21:3b).

Recently I've been meditating a lot on Revelation 3:20: "Behold, I stand at the door and knock. If anyone hears my voice and opens the door, I will come in to him and eat with him, and he with me."

It's a crazy thought that right now, even as you read this, Jesus is knocking on the door, desiring to sit and eat with you. I love this image of sharing a meal, lingering and fellowshipping with Him. Many years ago, a chef invited Lisa and me to his French restaurant. He asked us to sit and relax while he brought us different items to taste. Anyone who knows me knows that I love good food—especially when it's free. Every few minutes, he would come out of the kitchen with a different dish. He specifically brought small portions so we could enjoy more things. It was so fun to just sit with Lisa, talking and laughing, while being served great food. When dessert finally came out, we noticed that we had been there for nearly three hours! This is the kind of meal that Jesus wants to have with us—not hurried, just a prolonged enjoyable feast.

This communion is what we were made for. This is why St. Augustine said, "You have made us for yourself, O Lord, and our hearts are restless until they rest in you."* This is why the Westminster Catechism teaches that man's chief end is to glorify God and enjoy Him forever.

His nearness has to be our greatest treasure. We get worried and distracted by so many things, but only one thing is necessary. We need to be like Mary, who chose the better portion of sitting at Jesus' feet, or David, who says, "One thing have I asked of the LORD, that will I seek after: that I may dwell in the house of the LORD all the days of my life, to gaze upon the beauty of the LORD and to inquire in his temple" (Psalm 27:4).

I used to think these were just pretty words. Almost poetic hyperbole. "One thing"? Really, David? Not safety from your enemies? Not success in battle? Not the welfare of your family? Just dwelling in God's house? The older I get, the more I understand that David was not exaggerating.

---

* Augustine, *Confessions*, trans. Henry Chadwick (Oxford: Oxford University Press, 1991), 3.

Those who have tasted the sweetness of focused time in His presence know that it is the one thing that actually satisfies our souls.

Abiding in Love

Remember, we have an enemy who hates when we are in right relationship with God and is doing everything he can to impede our intimacy. This is why Jesus says in John 15:9, "As the Father has loved me, so have I loved you. Abide in my love."

To abide means to dwell or live inside of. Believing Jesus' love is not a one-time acknowledgement. It is a sustained connection. I have Christian friends who were once alcoholics or drug addicts. Some of them were completely delivered from both the sin and the temptation when they became believers. Others battle their temptations daily by the power of the Holy Spirit. God's grace doesn't always manifest the same, but it is always sufficient.

This seems to be the way it works with doubt. I have met people who are completely secure in God's love. They were delivered from insecurity at salvation and have never doubted His love for them. Others, like me, have to remind themselves daily of His promises. The enemy keeps shooting arrows of doubt at us. We have to constantly run for shelter. We are protected so long as we are abiding in His house.

The apostle Paul wrote a letter "to the saints who are in Ephesus, and are faithful in Christ Jesus" (Ephesians 1:1b). He is clearly addressing Christians, yet he tells them that he has been on his knees praying that "Christ may dwell in your hearts through faith" (3:17a).

Wait! Why? Isn't that the definition of a Christian? Weren't we told that Christ came into our hearts at salvation? Does He leave?

Paul goes on to pray that the Ephesian saints would "know the love of Christ" (3:19a).

Again, why would he have to pray that Christians would know the love of Christ? Is there such a thing as a faithful saint who doesn't know God's love?

A key clue is given in 3:18: "that you ... may have strength to comprehend ... what is the breadth and length and height and depth."

We don't often think about this, but part of our ongoing sanctification process is knowing His love. God wants us to explore the depths of His love. We often treat His love as a fact we accepted long ago. I believe God loves me, so I can check that box. Now it's time to move on and learn other truths, deeper truths. That way of thinking is so destructive. We are not meant to move on! We are meant to abide in His love. We abide by spending the rest of our lives learning how wide, long, high, and deep.

Why We Don't Abide

Looking back on my life, I don't believe that I didn't *believe* some of these truths about the love of God. I think I just didn't *think* about them. For many of us, we don't enjoy the love of God because we refuse to meditate on it. Some personality types struggle more with meditation than others, but we live in a time when everyone struggles. There are many reasons for this, but some common ones to consider are:

Distraction

Gone are the days when all the kids in the classroom pay attention except that one kid who can't seem to focus. The attentive kid is the anomaly now. These days, we are so inundated with information and stimulation that our minds are conditioned to keep moving on to the next thing. Videos and advertisements keep getting shorter, punchier, and louder to try to capture our increasingly limited attention spans. Our minds are so busy with all the media we consume, it's almost as if we are drunk or on a constant caffeine high. It's no wonder that when we come to meditate, it feels impossible. Our minds are clouded and our focus is weak, so we give up.

I remember my daughter telling me about how one of her college professors asked her class to practice sitting silently alone with the Lord for seven minutes each morning, and almost everyone confessed that they couldn't do it. They needed to turn on music to distract themselves or couldn't resist the urge to check their phones. If we can't sit still and focus for *seven minutes*, how are we ever going to sustain a relationship with a God that we can't see? A God who demands that we seek Him with our whole heart?

Silence and meditation are very important spiritual disciplines that are getting utterly lost in the American church today. If you find yourself unable to be quiet for any length of time, you urgently need to start working out that spiritual muscle. The enemy has popularized the inability to meditate, and God is calling us to rebel. This is not a light matter—I truly believe it is critical to the longevity of your faith. We all know that if you stop spending time with someone, it creates distance in the relationship. And a distant, shallow relationship with God is a playground for the enemy.

In Mark 1, we see Jesus' example:

> Very early in the morning, while it was still dark, Jesus got up, left the house and went off to a solitary place, where he prayed. Simon and his companions went to look for him, and when they found him, they exclaimed: "Everyone is looking for you!" (verses 35–37 NIV)

There are many other times in the gospel where it talks about Jesus doing whatever it took to get time alone with the Father. I'm sure many of the people who were looking for Jesus had important reasons. For some of those who were seeking healing, it could have been a matter of life and death. And yet, Jesus knew that He had to protect that time of communion with the Father. How often do we forsake communion with the Father for far less important reasons?

If you want to have a robust, intimate prayer life, you are going to have to sacrifice for it, and you are going to have to work at it. But there is no pursuit more worthy or rewarding!

Oh, taste and see that the LORD is good!
Blessed is the man who takes refuge in
him! (Psalm 34:8)

Problems

Some of us are natural problem solvers. Problem solvers tend to get consumed with the issue at hand and defer everything else until later. Meditating on love feels like a pleasure or luxury that you can get to once you've dealt with the more urgent matters. I know that personally, when someone attacks me or something goes wrong, my tendency is to meditate on that rather than keeping my eyes fixed on Christ.

In the famous Psalm 23 where David says, "The LORD is my shepherd; I shall not want," he goes on to say, "You prepare a table before me in the presence of my enemies" (verses 1, 5a).

There are other psalms where David asks God to defeat all his enemies or celebrates God's deliverance. But here David is saying, even in the *presence* of enemies, God prepares a table just to sit and be with him.

Years ago, I was in an elder meeting when the church was going through a difficult time. Our typical strategy would be to extend the meeting so we could have a longer discussion. One of the elders suggested that we should spend the entire time on our knees instead—trust our prayers more than our logic. It was hard to argue with that, even though everything in our flesh wanted to talk and fix the problems. We decided to forgo talking and just pray the entire time. I honestly don't recall the outcome, but I do remember leaving the room with peace. The best part about it was that we started a new trend. We endured too many meetings where discussion went overtime, leaving only a minute or two for a token closing prayer. It's no longer unusual for praise and prayer to go so long that we are left with little time for talking. I believe a day will come when God will show us how much time we wasted on earth "figuring things out" and reveal to us the outrageous results of our prayers.

Productivity

Some of us are addicted to accomplishment. Meditating on love doesn't feel productive, so it makes more sense to do something. In fact, some of you have skipped or skimmed every meditative exercise in this book so far because you are more concerned with finishing it than sitting with it. Caught you, didn't I?

But when Paul prays for the church in Ephesus, he asks that they would "know the love of Christ that surpasses knowledge, that you may be filled with all the fullness of God" (Ephesians 3:19).

Obviously, if I am filled with all the fullness of God, I am going to be effective for His kingdom. If you have to bet on someone working as hard as they can or someone who is filled with the fullness of God, you're going to go with the latter every time. And it may feel counterintuitive, but Paul is saying that knowing the love of Christ is what causes us to be filled with the fullness of God. My logic would tell me that I need to do something to be filled, but Scripture says differently. It's a matter of receiving His love.

David says, "O LORD, my heart is not lifted up; my eyes are not raised too high; I do not occupy myself with things too great and too marvelous for me. But I have calmed and quieted my soul, like a weaned child with its mother; like a weaned child is my soul within me" (Psalm 131:1–2).

In a frantic and dissatisfied world, God wants His children at rest. This doesn't mean we sit around and do nothing. Ephesians 2:10 says, "We are his workmanship, created in Christ Jesus for good works, *which God prepared beforehand*, that we should walk in them." God knows that you want your life to count, so you don't have to worry about it. He has plans for you. Rest in Him.

One thing that leads to unrest is our tendency to occupy ourselves "with things too great and marvelous." The arrogance of our hearts causes us to aspire to things above our paygrade. The internet is filled with people who believe they have the answer or they are the answer. King David quieted his soul "like a weaned child with its mother." Childlike faith requires childlike rest.

There were times in my life when my eyes were set on firing up the lukewarm church, ending world hunger, abolishing sex trafficking, uniting the church ... But as I get older and draw closer to the finish line, my ultimate dream doesn't revolve around accomplishments. At the end of my life, I want to be radically in love with the person of Jesus, fully secure in my identity as His beloved. And I want to spend the rest of my days here on earth doing what I will one day do forever: basking in and overflowing with the love of God. As I pursue Him, the accomplishments will come. If I frantically strive for accomplishments, I will have neither.

Failure

The enemy hates when the children of God rest securely in His love. He will do everything he can to sow thoughts of doubt and insecurity in your mind. He will relentlessly remind you of your failures so you will question God's ability to love a sinner as wretched as yourself. He will use other Christians to discourage you by broadcasting your failures. The deceiver will use any means to keep you living in shame. He'll even cause you to think you're being humble by meditating on your past failures!

Years ago, some of my friends got into mountain biking and asked if I wanted to try it. I was in decent shape and somewhat coordinated, so I figured I would have a good time. It didn't take long before I was sprawled out on the dirt with my bike on top of me. My "friends" had several good laughs at my many falls before one of them actually helped me. He asked if I was looking at the obstacles I was trying to avoid. He then explained that if I see a big rock, a crack in the ground, or a cliff, I can't stare at it. By looking at the obstacles, my body will naturally steer me toward them. The way to avoid those things is by picking a good path and staring only at the right path. This is such an important life lesson! If we keep looking at our failures, we're bound to repeat them. This is why we are told to fix our eyes on Jesus (see Hebrews 12:2). We would do well to heed the advice of Robert Murray McCheyne: "For every look at yourself, take ten looks at Christ."[†]

[†]   Andrew A. Bonar, *Memoir and Remains of the Rev. Robert Murray M'Cheyne, Minister of St. Peter's Church, Dundee* (Edinburgh: Oliphant Anderson & Ferrier, 1894), 293.

I don't mean at all that we should have a casual attitude toward sin. It is true that our sin grieves God, and it is right to feel the weight of that. But it also grieves God when we are slow to receive the forgiveness that He so readily offers. There is a subtle but very important distinction between conviction from the Holy Spirit and condemnation from the devil. Conviction produces repentance (see 2 Corinthians 7:10) and ultimately increases our love as we receive and rejoice in God's forgiveness (see Luke 7:47). Condemnation leads to a vicious cycle of shame, self-loathing, and death. When you find yourself getting sucked into that demonic cycle, take your eyes off of yourself and look at Jesus. Meditate on His character and take refuge in His mercy.

> But you are a God ready to forgive, gracious and merciful, slow to anger and abounding in steadfast love.... (Nehemiah 9:17b)

> If we confess our sins, he is faithful and just to forgive us our sins and to cleanse us from all unrighteousness. (1 John 1:9)

> For as high as the heavens are above the earth, so great is his steadfast love toward those who fear him; as far as the east is from the west, so far does

he remove our transgressions from
us. As a father shows compassion
to his children, so the LORD shows
compassion to those who fear him.
For he knows our frame; he remembers
that we are dust. (Psalm 103:11–14)

In the words of the 19th century hymn:

> Oh to grace how great a debtor
> Daily I'm constrained to be
> Let thy goodness, like a fetter
> Bind my wandering heart to thee

> Prone to wander, Lord, I feel it
> Prone to leave the God I love
> Here's my heart, oh take and seal it
> Seal it for thy courts above

Practical Advice for Abiding

By now, you have probably noticed tendencies in your
life that keep you from remaining in His love. Don't stop
there. Too many Christians are experts at conviction but
failures at action. By the Spirit, we all have the power to
make the changes that lead to life. We just have to choose
to put in the effort.

Take Thoughts Captive

In 1 Corinthians 6:19b–20, Paul tells the church, "You are not your own, for you were bought with a price. So glorify God in your body." Jesus purchased you with His blood, so you are no longer free to do whatever you want with your body. Most of us know our bodies are not meant to be used for evil, but do we apply the same principle to our minds? Paul tells the Philippians that they are not free to just think about anything. He gives criteria. Look through the following list of adjectives. Do your thoughts fit within these parameters?

> Finally, brothers, whatever is true, whatever is honorable, whatever is just, whatever is pure, whatever is lovely, whatever is commendable, if there is any excellence, if there is anything worthy of praise, think about these things. (verse 4:8)

So much of the battle to abide takes place in the mind. Years ago, a friend of mine had some terrible lies written and spoken about him. It was so staggering that he couldn't stop replaying those words in his mind. I had to remind him that as believers, we aren't permitted to do that. We have given our minds to God, and He tells us that these minds must only dwell on things that are *true, pure, lovely, praiseworthy...* We aren't free to replay lies or insults spoken against us. Our minds belong to Jesus. He wants our minds dwelling on Him, as He is the only One who truly fits the criteria of Philippians 4:8. We live in a fallen world. We can't control what we encounter, but we can control what we continue to think about.

Stop Consuming Junk

Think back to that picture of Jesus longing to sit and eat with you. Imagine that He has prepared an incredible feast for you to enjoy, with delicious food that contains all of the nutrients your body craves. This is our spiritual reality. But sadly, far too often we show up to the feast so full of junk we can hardly manage a couple bites of all that Jesus has prepared for us.

I recently read that the average teen spends almost eight hours a day playing games or consuming content on their phones. That's crazy! That's a full-time job. No wonder our spiritual senses are dulled and our appetite for God is nonexistent. We keep filling our minds and souls up with junk. A couple of times I have made it a rule for my kids that they could only be on electronics for the amount of time that they had spent in the Word or in prayer. Try it sometime—come to terms with the sheer number of hours that you spend mindlessly consuming. Cultivating a hunger for God's presence and power in your life might mean starving yourself of lesser things.

My friend Adam made a deal with his kids. If they would commit to going through high school without a smartphone, he would buy them any car they wanted on their sixteenth birthday! Most of us can't afford to do that (he was a pro athlete), but my point is that he got creative in keeping his kids off screens. What's exciting is that I'm noticing more and more young people choosing to ditch their smartphones. They are tired of constantly being tempted by pornography or wasting hours on social media. I am noticing more homes that don't have TVs in their living rooms. It seems the Holy Spirit is leading God's children to break their addictions to draw closer to Him.

Could you go a day without your phone? A week without social media? Two hours without checking your email? Try it, I dare you. These sound like impossible challenges to many of us, but they shouldn't be. And if they are, it might indicate that we've developed unhealthy dependencies that are crowding out our ability to genuinely abide in Christ.

Find Your Rhythm

The internet is flooded with dance routines. We love watching a group of people who can dance with perfect timing and well-choreographed moves. This was God's hope for Israel and the church. We were supposed to be a group with rhythm. God instituted rhythms of feasts and sacrifices to help His people keep themselves anchored in truth. He instituted Passover so that every year the Israelites would spend a week remembering how He brought them out of Egypt with a mighty hand and outstretched arm. He instituted the Sabbath so that each week the Israelites would rest and remember that "in six days the LORD made heaven and earth, the sea, and all that is in them, and rested on the seventh day. Therefore the LORD blessed the Sabbath day and made it holy" (Exodus 20:11). He instituted animal sacrifices to cleanse the people and remind them that the wages of sin is death.

In the early church days, the bells would ring at fixed times each day to cue believers to stop and pray the Lord's prayer. Orthodox believers continue the practice of daily prayer hours. How might our lives change if multiple times a day we stopped to cry out with millions of other believers to "Our Father"? How might the world change if the unified church fervently petitioned for His will to be done on earth as it is in heaven?

Every day I try to remind myself of two things: God is holy, and He loves me. I want the whole thrust of my life to rest on those two truths, so I have made a simple habit of speaking them over myself daily. Because I have been meditating on Revelation 3:20 so much recently, when I come to pray before a meal now, I picture Him wanting to sit and eat with me. Every mealtime is an opportunity to recognize His presence with me and enjoy that fellowship.

Last year our church did a series on Ephesians, and I challenged the congregation to pray Ephesians 1:15–23 over every member of their home group by name each day for a week. One of our pastors continued the practice for months.

I once read, "Moral agency repeated becomes moral character." The little decisions we make, our small daily rhythms, have huge spiritual implications for who we end up becoming. These days, many evangelicals are wary of anything liturgical or ritualistic because we associate it with "dead religion" or legalism, and it certainly can become that. But done in faith and with intentionality, rhythms of prayer and practice can make it so that our everyday life is grounded in worship. Without rhythm, life easily becomes scattered and compartmentalized, and we miss out on all these opportunities to abide in and enjoy Him.

We all have times where we get convicted or excited about something, but it doesn't ultimately lead to change. If what you have read so far has struck a chord with you, that's great, but I encourage you to take it a step further. Before you continue on to the next chapter, spend some time praying about what tangible changes you can make to ensure you don't just move off of this topic in the months and years to come.

Only as we abide in Him, only as we marinate in His love, can we truly live out our identity as His beloved children and radiant bride. It's not enough to know who we are; we must live from that place of secure identity. And that happens one day at a time, one moment at a time, as we choose to turn our hearts toward Him and receive His never-ending love.

V.

CHAPTER FIVE

OVERFLOW

A s I have been teaching on how to rest securely in the love of Jesus, it may sound like I'm contradicting everything I wrote in *Crazy Love*. The point of that book was to address the fact that the Christianity of the New Testament looks extremely different from what we were experiencing in the U.S. We attend church services that make us feel comfortable when Jesus commanded us to deny ourselves, pick up our cross, and follow Him. My fear while I wrote the book was that we resembled the lukewarm church of Laodicea in Revelation 3. In love, I was hoping to stir people's convictions because I didn't want them to be spit out of the mouth of God.

> I know your works: you are neither cold
> nor hot. Would that you were either cold
> or hot! So, because you are lukewarm,
> and neither hot nor cold, I will spit you
> out of my mouth. For you say, I am rich, I
> have prospered, and I need nothing, not
> realizing that you are wretched, pitiable,
> poor, blind, and naked. (verses 15–17)

I literally get frightened when I read passages like this as well as the other loving warnings in Scripture. It seems in the end there will be many who are deceived. Like those mentioned above, they are "not realizing" that they are "wretched, pitiable, poor, blind, and naked." These are not words that describe believers. Being spit out of the mouth of God does not describe the fate of believers. Yet, I meet many believers who casually joke about being lukewarm as though it's not a big deal! My views on these passages have not changed. I still can't see the logic in the term "lukewarm Christian." It's an oxymoron.

I don't regret writing *Crazy Love*. I just wish I had written this book first. If we don't believe, receive, and meditate on the love of God regularly, the message of *Crazy Love* can lead people into frantic works. It's not that I didn't mention the love of Christ in the book; I just didn't emphasize it enough. That was the meaning of the arrows on the cover. It was to symbolize God's love coming down to us before our love can be shown to Him. But I didn't write much about His love because I honestly didn't think about it that much.

Before settling on *Beloved*, my original plan was to title this book *Crazy Loved*. I wanted everyone who read my first book to know my change in perspective in hopes that they might experience something similar. I went back and forth in choosing a title, but ultimately felt it was safer to go with a biblical term. It also summarizes what so many struggle with. For many, the hardest thing to do is be loved.

I want to clarify that I am not trying to water down the message in *Crazy Love*. This is not an effort to temper your works in order to make room for receiving love. On the contrary, my understanding of Scripture is that it is God's love for us that enables us to do far more sacrificial and extravagant works than through our own willpower.

We can't forget God's solution for the lukewarm church in Laodicea.

> I counsel you to buy from me gold refined by fire, so that you may be rich, and white garments so that you may clothe yourself and the shame of your nakedness may not be seen, and salve to anoint your eyes, so that you may see. Those whom I love, I reprove and discipline, so be zealous and repent. Behold, I stand at the door and knock. If anyone hears my voice and opens the door, I will come in to him and eat with him, and he with me. (Revelation 3:18–20)

He does tell us to "be zealous and repent." This passage is not merely passive. There should be a repentance motivated by the fear of being spit out of the mouth of God. The key, however, is the very next phrase: "Behold, I stand at the door and knock." He is telling the church that He is banging on the door, asking us to let Him in. He wants to eat with us and give us true riches, clean garments, and true sight for our eyes.

If we keep working out of our own power, we will only produce lukewarm results no matter how hard we try. Have you ever answered the door, sat at the table with Him, and actually asked Him to give you true riches, clothe you in white garments, and open your eyes? Some of us grow up in traditions that make everything figurative.

Maybe being zealous means you literally set up a table, believe in God's presence with you, and ask. Literally confess that your own efforts leave you lukewarm, poor, blind, pitiable, and naked. Literally tell your Savior that you want "gold refined by fire, so that you may be rich, and white garments so that you may clothe yourself and the shame of your nakedness may not be seen, and salve to anoint your eyes, so that you may see."

Which Came First? Love or Obedience? His Love or Mine?

For decades, I looked at John 14:15 as a cause and effect statement. It is, but I had the cause and effect backwards. It reads, "If you love me, you will keep my commandments."

When I pondered that passage, my response was to work hard at obeying His commands to prove to God and myself that I really do love Him. In other words, if I keep His commands, it will cause Him to love me. What Jesus is teaching is the same as "we love because he first loved us" (1 John 4:19). Because He loved us, and because we believe and abide in His love, it results in obedience. It's not something that we need to muster up. His radical, undying love for us is a scalding hot truth. When rightly understood, it will not yield a lukewarm response. The more we grow in love, the more "the things of earth will grow strangely dim."* Our obsession, satisfaction, and enjoyment of His love leaves us longing to pour our lives out at His feet.

Motive Matters

I've been in ministry for almost forty years, and recently I was looking back and thinking through how many

---

* Helen Howarth Lemmel, "Turn Your Eyes Upon Jesus," in Glad Songs (London: Pickering & Inglis, 1922).

things in my lifetime were truly done out of this overflow of love, and how many things I just did because it was my job, or because I felt guilty or wanted to prove myself. I've done a lot of right things, but a lot of it wasn't for the right reasons.

1 Corinthians 13:1–3 says, "If I speak in the tongues of men and of angels, but have not love, I am a noisy gong or a clanging cymbal. And if I have prophetic powers, and understand all mysteries and all knowledge, and if I have all faith, so as to remove mountains, but have not love, I am nothing. If I give away all I have, and if I deliver up my body to be burned, but have not love, I gain nothing."

Anyone who has been serving in ministry for years knows how easy it is to just go through the motions. Pretty soon we are just doing stuff rather than loving people. I used to keep a list of questions in the front of my Bible that I would ask myself before preaching. Question number two was: Do I actually love these people? I needed this because it became natural for me to step on a stage and share a message while feeling nothing for the people to whom I was speaking. Oftentimes, I would hide backstage and look at people's faces. I would ask God to give me love for them and help me speak to them out of love. This kept me from merely teaching or giving a talk.

Earlier in the book we looked at Paul's prayer for the Ephesian church. He was on his knees praying that they would know the depths of God's love and be "rooted and grounded in love" (Ephesians 3:17b). Sadly, God addresses that church years later in Revelation 2:

> To the angel of the church in Ephesus write: "The words of him who holds the seven stars in his right hand, who walks among the seven golden lampstands.
>
> "I know your works, your toil and your patient endurance, and how you cannot bear with those who are evil, but have tested those who call themselves apostles and are not, and found them to be false. I know you are enduring patiently and bearing up for my name's sake, and you have not grown weary. But I have this against you, that you have abandoned the love you had at first. Remember therefore from where you have fallen; repent, and do the works you did at first. If not, I will come to you and remove your lampstand from its place, unless you repent." (verses 1–5)

They were still doing the right things, but they had abandoned their love. They weren't working out of the overflow of a loving relationship. What is striking about this passage is that God warns that He will remove the church altogether if they don't change (verse 5). When you look at the list of all the things they did right, it's shocking that God wouldn't want the church around. That's how much He values our love relationship. The tragedy of this passage is that it actually happens. Historians say the church ceased to exist shortly after Revelation was written, and there has been little to no church presence there for the past nineteen hundred years. Today, where Ephesus once stood is now a small city named Selçuk. It is in modern day Turkey which is 99.8 percent Muslim.

Works without love will end in numbness, burnout, and ultimately, destruction. 1 Corinthians 3 tells us that in the end, all of our works will be tested by fire (verses 12–13). It doesn't matter how impressive it looks—if love is not the foundation, our work is in vain.

The Only Right Motive

For the love of Christ controls us, because we
have concluded this: that one has died for all,
therefore all have died; and he died for all,

that those who live might no longer live for
themselves but for him who for their sake died
and was raised. (2 Corinthians 5:14–15)

Paul, talking about his ministry, explains the only right motive for ministry. That first phrase is translated in the New English Bible as, "The love of Christ leaves us with no choice." It's this idea of being so consumed by the love of Christ that it can't help but overflow out of us. It is similar to God being "rich in mercy" (Ephesians 2:4) and "abounding in steadfast love" (Exodus 34:6). The picture is of a God so full of love that it overflows. He is so rich in mercy that He creates beings to receive it. When we receive the love of God, it's like we become full to overflowing. As the psalmist says, "My cup overflows" (verse 23:5b). His love is more than we can contain.

Picture a wine glass being filled with the most expensive wine. The cup eventually overflows, and you panic because you can't bear the thought of it going to waste. You want someone else to capture it and enjoy it as you have. We are intended to enjoy His love, but that can't be the end of the story. Until His love flows through us, it's incomplete. This is exactly what 1 John 4:12 explains: "No one has ever seen God; if we love one another, God abides in us and his love is perfected in us."

If we love one another, we have proof that *God abides in us.* How do you know that God is truly abiding in you? You love your brothers and sisters. He uses the word *perfected* again in verses 17–18: "By this is love perfected with us, so that we may have confidence for the day of judgment, because as he is so also are we in this world. There is no fear in love, but perfect love casts out fear. For fear has to do with punishment, and whoever fears has not been perfected in love."

This is powerful—don't miss it! It is only when His love is *perfected* that the fear of judgment is completely removed. His love is perfected in us when we love one another. When we abide in His love, it motivates us to become like Him—"as he is so also are we in this world." It's a simple formula where one thing results in the next:

We abide in His love
↓
We love one another
↓
His love is perfected in us
↓
All fear of judgment is gone

While there is a monastic side to us that longs to be away from people and alone with God, there is also a missional side to us that longs to impart this pleasure to others. We are unable to sit idly. The best picture I can think of is when our fifth child was born. Claire immediately had two parents and four siblings showering her with love. While it was beautiful, it also felt unbalanced. Lisa began thinking how crazy it was that this little baby was almost being smothered with attention while others received none. This is what led us to foster and adopt. Our love for Claire was overflowing. We had too much love to share.

One of the most beautiful things about loving others sacrificially or even suffering to share the gospel is that you don't have to pause your communion with God to do so. In fact, some of my greatest moments of intimacy have come in the midst of sacrifice or suffering for the gospel. After all, Jesus said that He would be with us "always, to the end of the age" (Matthew 28:20b) in the context of making disciples. It was when Shadrach, Meshach, and Abednego were thrown into a fire that a fourth person manifested before them (see Daniel 3:23–24). It was as Stephen was being stoned to death that he looked into the sky and saw Jesus (see Acts 7:55)! It's an amazing cycle that we get to be a part of: our intimacy with Christ compels us to minister, and as we minister, we experience an even greater intimacy with Christ!

The Overflow

Remember that wine glass being filled with wine? Picture it again. When God's love fills us to the point of overflowing, what spills out is radical love for others. Let me show you what this overflow looks like in real life.

Radical Love for the Body

A new commandment I give to you, that you
love one another: just as I have loved you, you
also are to love one another. (John 13:34)

After spending the last couple of chapters meditating on the magnitude and wonder of God's love, I hope this calling feels more weighty to you. Just as it's crazy to think that Jesus says *as* the Father has loved me, so have I loved you, it's crazy to think that *as* He has loved us, so we are to love one another.

I have been loved so deeply by so many members of the church. It fascinates me that in every city I've visited, I have found Christians who are eager to bless me in some fashion. It only occurred to me recently that they were sent by God. This is one of the main ways that God shows His love. It's through the church. For years, I have felt blessed by Christians, but I somehow separated that from God. I now see that they love me because God loves me. He sent them to love me in His name.

His intention is for us to not just be loved by Him, but by His church body. After all, we are members of His body.

For so many who didn't grow up being loved by family, the church was meant to more than make up for that.

I was eighteen years old with nowhere to live when Mike and Vicky took me into their home. They had only been married a couple of years and had a baby girl. They hardly knew me, but they knew I needed a place to stay. Far from merely giving me a room to sleep in, they made me feel like a part of their family. Who does that? At that point in my walk, I didn't know the church was supposed to be a family. Looking back, I can see God was pouring His grace out on me. Most people know theologically that the church should love like a family, but they never experience it. Maybe some of our doubt in God's love comes from the lack of love we've received from His body. We shouldn't be doing this alone. We're incomplete. It's when we're together that we most fully experience His love.

"In him you also are being built together into a dwelling place for God by the Spirit" (Ephesians 2:22).

I enjoy being alone with God. I have experienced His love while taking long walks on the beach, in the wilderness, and alone in my prayer room. It's definitely counterintuitive to think that I would experience His presence and love when surrounded by a group of people, but that is what Paul is saying here. He alludes to the building of the temple in the Old Testament. When every piece is in place, God comes down and inhabits the temple. Here he says that we "are being built together into a dwelling place for God"! There is some mysterious way that God's presence dwells with us when we are *together*.

Have you ever experienced this? Do you have a circle of believers whom you know and love deeply? When you gather to praise Jesus with other committed followers whom you love, something supernatural happens. As 1 John 4:12 says, "His love is perfected in us." This only takes place when we are loving one another. It's not enough to be loved by a group of people, and it's not enough if you're the only one loving. We must "love one another" (verse 11b). This is why it's foolish to say, "I love Jesus but not the church." You can't know the fullness of God's love apart from the body.

Radical Love for the Poor

A few years ago, I was speaking with a woman who told me that for years, she and her spiritual leader, Jorge, ministered weekly in the slums. Jorge would remind her regularly to do more than pass out food. "Love them and embrace them. How could you pass up a chance to hug Jesus?" As she reflected on those precious times in the slums, she explained her mixed emotions when her dear friend was chosen to be the next pope. She knew that once

Jorge became Pope Francis, she would no longer enjoy walking alongside him to encounter Jesus in the slums.

> Then the righteous will answer him, saying, "Lord, when did we see you hungry and feed you, or thirsty and give you drink? And when did we see you a stranger and welcome you, or naked and clothe you? And when did we see you sick or in prison and visit you?" And the King will answer them, "Truly, I say to you, as you did it to one of the least of these my brothers, you did it to me."
> (Matthew 25:37–40)

Jesus doesn't just care about the poor—He identifies with them. He places Himself in their position. And when we ignore them, we ignore Him.

Think about it: the Creator of the universe chose to be born into poverty, not wealth. He could have come as a king with palaces and servants, but instead was laid in a feeding trough by parents who could only afford the poorest person's sacrifice at the temple—two small birds. He had "nowhere to lay his head" during His ministry (Matthew 8:20b). And at the end, He died naked, possessing nothing, not even the clothes on His back.

This is our God—one who doesn't just sympathize with the poor from a distance but enters into their suffering completely. And if we claim to love Him, how can we not love those He so closely identifies with?

When I first visited Ethiopia, I walked through homes built from scraps, saw children drink water that made them sick, and met mothers who couldn't feed their babies. Weeping in my hotel room, I finally understood James 2:5a "Has not God chosen those who are poor in the world to be rich in faith and heirs of the kingdom...?"

I realized it wasn't about us helping them—it was about us learning to see Jesus in places we'd been trained to ignore. The poor aren't a project; they're precious to God. They're not a category; they're Christ in disguise.

Every time I reach out to touch a weathered hand or look into eyes dulled by suffering, I'm reaching toward Jesus. When I give to someone in need, I'm not being charitable—I'm responding to my Savior who said, "I was hungry and you gave me food" (Matthew 25:35a).

This isn't optional for those who love Jesus. It's impossible to truly abide in His love and remain unmoved by what moves His heart. The question isn't "Should I care for the poor?" but rather "How can I claim to love Jesus and not love those He identifies with so closely?"

My wife sometimes tells the story of when I came home from my first trip to Africa. I was so shocked and saddened by the extreme poverty, I was itching to do something. I told her we needed to downsize our home and give away the excess. At the time, she didn't understand. Giving away half of our possessions and squeezing our growing family into a much smaller place felt like a heavy sacrifice. But to her credit, she submitted even when she didn't understand. She trusted me enough to take the leap of faith.

Years later, I finally took her with me to Africa. After seeing the orphans, holding the children, meeting the widows, she turned to me and said, "I wish we had given more!" The experience of seeing need firsthand transformed her heart in the same way it had mine. And what began as a reluctant sacrifice became one of the greatest joys of our lives. Now we get updates about children who are thriving, communities that have clean water, families that are intact—and the joy we feel is indescribable.

That's what happens when God's love overflows through us. What starts as obedience becomes delight.

Radical Love for the Lost

One of the most sobering realities for me has been realizing just how many people around the world have never heard the name of Jesus. Billions of people have never once been told about the God who loves them so much that He sent His only Son to die for them. As I've meditated more on God's love for me, I've found myself increasingly burdened for those who don't know that love.

I remember sitting with a couple in Myanmar who had never heard about Jesus. As I asked questions about their lives, I discovered that they were both diagnosed with cancer. They were sitting in a makeshift tent in the slums just waiting to die. As I shared the gospel with them through a translator, they seemed receptive to everything I was saying. I prayed with them and I kept praying for them during my flight home. A few months later, I reconnected with my friend who translated for me that day. He told me that he visited that same couple weeks later and they asked him, "Why did you wait so long to visit us again? We want to get baptized!"

That story thrills me and haunts me. How many others are out there, living in fear, desperation, and despondence, never having heard that there is a God who loves them perfectly and offers an eternal hope? If we really believe in God's love, how can we not be compelled to share it?

The love of Christ doesn't just make us feel good—it controls us, compels us, leaves us with no choice but to live for the One who died for us. And living for Him means sharing His heart for the lost, His desire that none should perish but that all should come to repentance.

Radical Joy

> *In all things I have shown you that by*
> *working hard in this way we must help*
> *the weak and remember the words of the*
> *Lord Jesus, how he himself said, "It is more*
> *blessed to give than to receive." (Acts 20:35)*

For months, my son Zeke asked me if I would buy him a drum set. I kept telling him that our house was too small and the drums would be too loud. Then came his birthday ... I'm so bummed that I didn't record his reaction when he walked into his bedroom and saw a full drum kit! He screamed, fell on the floor, and then jumped into my arms. He was so happy he didn't even know what to do with himself, so he started flopping around on the floor in excitement. It was so fun to watch a human being express so much happiness and then realize that I caused it!

It is better to give than to receive! The experience of giving love is better than that of receiving. Recently, a woman came up to me with a huge smile and couldn't stop telling me how happy she was. That week, she had prayed for the first time and God answered her! When I met her a few weeks prior to this joyous encounter, she was sad, weeping, unsure if

God existed. Now she is a baptized follower of Jesus and beloved member of our church. God took a woman who grew up in a communist country and showed her the love of a heavenly Father. And I got to be a part of that!

Around the same time, I received a picture from Ethiopia. My eyes immediately welled up with tears. It was a teenage girl with a radiant smile, and her eyes were absolutely beaming. I realized it was the same girl I met eleven years before when she was literally skin and bones with days, maybe only hours, to live. Now she is a beautiful young woman who worships Jesus. And I got to be a part of that!

I honestly can't imagine a more fulfilling use of my time or money. God's commandments are not burdensome—they really do lead to life! I want to be clear that in saying we need to be compelled by love, I am not saying that we should only obey when we feel like it. Sometimes loving one another deeply gets hard, and that is not an excuse to quit. Sometimes God will ask you to give until it hurts.

But as He fills us with more of His love, and we fall deeper in love with Him, it empowers us to follow even when we don't understand. Because He is a good King, His commandments lead us to life, and it becomes this holy cycle of receiving riches and joyfully casting them back at His feet.

And whenever the living creatures give glory and honor and thanks to him who is seated on the throne, who lives forever and ever, the twenty-four elders fall down before him who is seated on the throne and worship him who lives forever and ever. They cast their crowns before the throne, saying,

"Worthy are you, our Lord and God,
to receive glory and honor and power,
for you created all things, and by your
will they existed and were created."
(Revelation 4:9–11)

That's our destiny—to be so captivated by His glory, so overwhelmed by His love, that we can't help but cast everything we have at His feet. And the beautiful thing is, we don't have to wait for heaven to begin living this way. We can start now, today, by opening our hearts to His love and letting it overflow to everyone around us.

VI.

CHAPTER SIX

ENDURANCE

A nd because lawlessness will be increased, the love of many will grow cold. But the one who endures to the end will be saved. (Matthew 24:12–13)

Jesus tells us exactly what will happen in the end—sin will increase and love will decrease. He shares this as a warning, but also to encourage His beloved to endure. In forty years of pastoring, I have seen hundreds of people walk away from Him. I am sure that many of you have experienced the same heartbreak of watching someone you love or someone that you used to look up to lose their first love. In this chapter, my hope is to strengthen and encourage you to be one of those who endure. To that end, I want to identify three primary forces that are working against you and point you to the tools we have been given to hold fast.

Obstacles to Living as the Beloved
Spiritual Entropy: Our Love Grows Cold
We don't like to admit it, but our natural tendency is toward spiritual entropy. We never simply drift into

greater love, greater unity, or greater holiness. Without the constant grace of God, our love for Him naturally cools.

This isn't just true spiritually—it's true of every relationship.

Lisa and I have watched so many couples fall in love. Initially, they couldn't get enough of each other. They would make every effort to clear their schedules just to be together. They could laugh and talk for hours about the stupidest things. Then they would get married and have kids and their jobs and lives became busier. Before they knew it, they were more like roommates than lovers. They weren't necessarily fighting but they definitely weren't connecting. Their love was cooling, and they didn't even notice.

This happens so subtly. You don't wake up one morning and decide "Today I'm going to stop loving Jesus." Instead, you get a little busier. Prayer gets shorter. Bible reading becomes sporadic. Church attendance becomes optional. Conversations about spiritual things become less frequent. And one day you realize that what was once a passionate love affair with Jesus has become a distant memory.

It is significant that Jesus says, "The love of many will grow cold" (Matthew 24:12b). We tend to get fixated on the immorality in the church, but that's merely the by-product of people losing their first love. The answer is not to join an accountability group or avoid tempting environments. Those things can be helpful, but our ultimate safety comes from staying in love.

I have spent many hours trying to convince couples on the brink of divorce to stay together. Sometimes their convictions are enough to survive another week, but they eventually quit. It's so hard to relate because I've never needed willpower to stay married. Quite the opposite, I've often wondered how miserable I would be if Lisa died or left me. It's not that we don't go through hard times, but I can't imagine life without her. After thirty-two years, our love keeps deepening. We are more in love than ever. This is the kind of relationship God wants to have with us.

For too many people, Christianity is all about fighting temptation and holding on to beliefs. They've never considered that it can be a relationship so enjoyable that they can't bear the thought of it ending.

Peter describes it like this: "Though you have not seen him, you love him. Though you do not now see him, you believe in him and rejoice with joy that is inexpressible and filled with glory" (1 Peter 1:8).

Peter is not being hyperbolic when he tells us we can experience joy that is inexpressible and filled with glory. He's not speaking as though it is something we should strive for; he assumes it is already happening!

Some of you grew up in church environments that were all about discipline, self-control, and denying yourself (all of which are biblical), but that's all you know of following Christ. While it is possible for your belief in Christ to endure by sheer discipline, it is not God's desire for you. Like a great marriage, He wants you to receive so much enjoyment from knowing Him that you can't bear the thought of it ever ending.

Remember the scene in John 6. Thousands of people are crowding around Jesus while He preaches a series of hard truths. By the time He is done, almost everyone has deserted Him. Jesus then looks at His twelve disciples and asks, "Do you want to go away as well?" (verse 67b). That's when Peter gives his epic response: "Lord, to whom shall we go? You have the words of eternal life, and we have believed, and have come to know, that you are the Holy One of God" (verses 68–69).

I hope your heart resonates with Peter's! How in the world could I ever leave Jesus now that I know who He is? How do I upgrade from the Holy One of God? Who else would I follow when He has the words of eternal life? I feel exactly like Peter feels. I can't imagine ever leaving Jesus!

Spiritual Isolation: The Danger of Going It Alone

I love a good campfire, and I like being the guy who starts it and keeps it burning. I get obsessed with positioning each piece of wood perfectly to get the maximum blaze. I can stare at a fire for hours. There's something about the way the logs glow as the fire intensifies—it's mesmerizing. Eventually, everybody heads off to bed and it's time for me to put out the fire. It's simple. All I have to do is separate the pieces of wood from each other. Amazing how quickly a blazing piece of wood can cool off just through isolation.

Dallas Willard once wrote, "Personalities united can contain more of God and sustain the force of His greater presence much better than scattered individuals."*

---

* Dallas Willard, *The Spirit of the Disciplines: Understanding How God Changes Lives* (New York: HarperSanFrancisco, 1999), 186.

We love being with Jesus, but that doesn't mean we are immune to discouragement. It must have been painful for the disciples to watch thousands of people walk away from Jesus. They must have had moments where they wondered if they were the ones who were wrong. There's nothing like being severely outnumbered to test the strength of your convictions.

It gets lonely when you watch friends walk away from Jesus and destroy their lives through adultery, substance abuse, suicide, and more. It is frustrating to watch ministers leave the ministry, leave the faith, or fall into sin. It's depressing to watch families devastated by divorce and churches decimated by ungodly leadership.

There is a disturbing new trend where people still label themselves Christian while embracing sin. Rather than leaving the church, they claim to be part of a progressive church with better theology. Like Satan in the garden, they constantly ask, "Did God actually say ...?" (Genesis 3:1). They claim that Christians have been wrong for two thousand years, and they are finally interpreting Scripture correctly. Historically, the church has always been opposed to homosexuality, divorce, abortion, or switching genders. Churches are now hesitant to address these issues for fear of being labeled unloving.

Absolute truth is being replaced by relativism, so you can just be spiritual however feels right to you. These are challenging times for those who hold to orthodox views.

Sometimes we feel completely alone when we stand on biblical truth. We need to remind ourselves that we are siding with millions of believers over thousands of years, and that there are currently millions of followers around the earth who are deeply committed and standing for truth despite heavy persecution.

We all love the story of Elijah on Mount Carmel battling 450 prophets of Baal by himself (1 Kings 18). God stood with Elijah, and answered Elijah's prayer to send fire from heaven. What was it like when he went to bed that night? He must have replayed that experience over and over in his mind. He must have thanked God a hundred times. God will call you to stand alone with Him at times, and those could become the most memorable times of your life. Our intimacy with God isn't developed only during quiet and meditation. It's when our faith is tested and we survive the heat of battle that we experience Him uniquely. It's when we walk through the valley of the shadow of death that we enjoy the presence of our good Shepherd most (Psalm 23).

Many of us are puzzled when we read the next chapter—
1 Kings 19. Elijah, who seemed invincible after defeating
the prophets of Baal, is now terrified and hiding in a cave
because a woman is chasing him.

> And behold, the word of the LORD came
> to him, and he said to him, "What are
> you doing here, Elijah?" He said, "I have
> been very jealous for the LORD, the God
> of hosts. For the people of Israel have
> forsaken your covenant, thrown down
> your altars, and killed your prophets
> with the sword, and I, even I only, am
> left, and they seek my life, to take it
> away." (verses 9–10)

Elijah is so discouraged and afraid, he is on the brink of
giving up. This is God's response:

> And the LORD said to him, "Go, return on
> your way to the wilderness of Damascus.
> And when you arrive, you shall anoint
> Hazael to be king over Syria. And Jehu
> the son of Nimshi you shall anoint to
> be king over Israel, and Elisha the son
> of Shaphat of Abel-meholah you shall

anoint to be prophet in your place. And the one who escapes from the sword of Hazael shall Jehu put to death, and the one who escapes from the sword of Jehu shall Elisha put to death. Yet I will leave seven thousand in Israel, all the knees that have not bowed to Baal, and every mouth that has not kissed him."
(verses 15–18)

Elijah's discouragement is from believing that he is the "only one left." God's response to Elijah is to "go." You're not finished yet. Go anoint the next generation of leaders and prophets. You are not the only one left—I have a remnant of seven thousand who have not bowed to Baal. While there are times when God gives us the courage to stand alone, there are other times when He encourages us by showing us that we have others with us.

Satan wants you to feel alone, discouraged, and weak. But the truth is, God will never leave you nor forsake you. And you are "fellow citizens with the saints and members of the household of God, built on the foundation of the apostles and prophets, Christ Jesus himself being the cornerstone, in whom the whole structure, being joined together, grows into a holy temple in the Lord. In him you also are being built together into a dwelling place for God by the Spirit" (Ephesians 2:19b–22).

I love this picture. Each of us are bricks in this living temple, joining together with every believer from the beginning of time—Abraham, Moses, Jeremiah, Paul, John, the early church fathers, all of the nameless people who have spent their lives for the glory of God. Christ Himself is the cornerstone, and God dwells in the midst of us.

I pray this fills you with so much hope and strength! Sometimes we can get so caught up in our own lives and circumstances, and we need to be reminded that we are part of this glorious eternal story. Though there may be isolated times when we will have to stand alone, God's plan is for us to stand together.

Have you ever locked arms with people in order to get across a rushing river? I've only done it once. Some of the people definitely would have been swept away by the current if they tried to cross individually, but our collective weight and footing allowed us to stay grounded and cross safely. It's a great picture of God's intention for the church. In Philippians 1:27–29 Paul talks about how we are supposed to strive "side by side for the faith of the gospel." This is how we remain "not frightened in anything." As Paul says, it is His plan that we "suffer for his sake," but we can stand firm if we stand together.

I'm blessed to be a part of a wonderful local church. We aren't big, but we love each other deeply. We are not perfect, but we are together. I rarely, if ever, feel alone. Thank God if you enjoy fellowship like this. If you are not a part of a church like this, you can be. It is usually not something you just effortlessly step into, but rather a community you help build. It's easy to stand back and point fingers at other people for not doing their part, but an idle, critical spirit is never going to lead to the loving unity you crave. Pray for it. In faith, expect answers and persevere in love: "Love one another with brotherly affection. Outdo one another in showing honor" (Romans 12:10).

Opposition: The Enemy Who Never Rests

If a guy fought a lion and the lion won, would you be surprised? We really shouldn't be surprised to see so many people currently losing to the enemy.

> Humble yourselves, therefore, under the mighty hand of God so that at the proper time he may exalt you, casting all

your anxieties on him, because he cares for you. Be sober-minded; be watchful. Your adversary the devil prowls around like a roaring lion, seeking someone to devour. (1 Peter 5:6–8)

Peter warns that the devil is always looking for opportunities to destroy you. At the same time, Peter also tells you that you don't need to be anxious at all. Why? You can rest "under the mighty hand of God ... because he cares for you." If we are going to survive, we need to stay aware of both realities.

Picture a lion seeking to devour you but the mighty hand of God protecting you because of His care for you. How often do you think about these truths? Both realities are happening right now. You have an enemy scheming to destroy your life. He wants to take your eyes off the God who cares for you. He wants you to doubt the power that's available to you.

Paul prays that the eyes of your heart would be enlightened to know "the immeasurable greatness of his power toward us who believe, according to the working of his great might that he worked in Christ when he raised him from the dead and seated him at his right hand in the heavenly places, far above all rule and authority and power and dominion, and above every name that is named, not only in this age but also in the one to come" (Ephesians 1:19–21).

We can stand in the same strength that raised Christ from the dead and seated Him on high. God fights for us, but He also calls us to lay hold of this strength and fight alongside Him. Many of us are not fighting because we don't take His words literally. We treat this battle figuratively—like it's a cute analogy. The war is spiritual, but that does not mean it is not literal! You are literally being targeted right now. Paul instructs the Ephesian church,

> Finally, be strong in the Lord and in the strength of his might. Put on the whole armor of God, that you may be able to stand against the schemes of the devil. For we do not wrestle against flesh and blood, but against the rulers, against the authorities, against the cosmic powers over this present darkness, against the spiritual forces of evil in the heavenly places. Therefore take up the whole armor of God, that

you may be able to withstand in the evil day, and having done all, to stand firm. Stand therefore, having fastened on the belt of truth, and having put on the breastplate of righteousness, and, as shoes for your feet, having put on the readiness given by the gospel of peace. In all circumstances take up the shield of faith, with which you can extinguish all the flaming darts of the evil one; and take the helmet of salvation, and the sword of the Spirit, which is the word of God, praying at all times in the Spirit, with all prayer and supplication. To that end, keep alert with all perseverance, making supplication for all the saints, and also for me, that words may be given to me in opening my mouth boldly to proclaim the mystery of the gospel, for which I am an ambassador in chains, that I may declare it boldly, as I ought to speak. (Ephesians 6:10–20)

You will die if you do not get serious about standing "in the strength of his might." You are destined to join the long list of those who have fallen unless you recognize the danger. There has only been one time in my life when I had to put on a bulletproof vest (don't ask). It's our natural instinct to protect ourselves when there is physical danger, so how come we don't protect ourselves in the face of spiritual danger? We have to take this spiritual war more seriously than we currently do.

Be honest—how often do you even think about the fact that you are in a war? When was the last time you actually fought? When was the last time you went through this list to see if you're properly armed? I could write a whole book about this passage, but let's just take a few things off the list.

Have you "fastened on the belt of truth"? All day every day, the demons are lying to you. They whisper lies directly into your ears, but they also do it through videos, songs, podcasts, friends, and church leaders. We must take those thoughts captive, destroying them and replacing them with truth. Saturate yourself with truth. Last year, I read through the Bible cover to cover twelve times. I wanted my mind so filled with truth that there would be no room for lies. I figured if I kept listening to the Shepherd's voice, I wouldn't hear the enemy's.

Have you taken up "the shield of faith"? If the enemy can't get us to believe lies, he will get us to doubt truth.

"Did God actually say" (Genesis 3:1) that He loves you? Intellectual knowledge of the truth is necessary but not sufficient. We must have faith in those truths. Faith is what can extinguish all the flaming darts of the evil one. This is why we meditate on the passages listed in chapter 2. We increase our faith in God's love for us by worshipping Him for His love.

Are you "making supplication for all the saints"? Remember, this is about us winning a war, not just you surviving it. The way that we pray for others must have some unique effect on this war, otherwise God would just have every saint pray for themselves.

Even as I write this, I am deeply convicted. If God were to write out all of the prayers I have prayed to Him this past year on behalf of other saints, I would be embarrassed. Most of us have spent more time judging, criticizing, and talking about fellow soldiers than we have spent praying for them. That is no way to fight a war.

My guess is that by thinking about just these three concepts, you see that you haven't been fighting the war very fiercely. Beloved, go back through the entire list in Ephesians 6. Arm yourself with all of the amazing weapons your loving Father has provided you.

Heaven

The last thing I want to leave you with is a vision of heaven. This is ultimately why we won't quit, no matter how brutal this battle gets. The end is near. Soon our lungs of flesh will take their last breath, and we will find ourselves before HIM.

Imagine that moment. Meditate on it. This is why we endure.

> Let not your hearts be troubled. Believe in God; believe also in me. In my Father's house are many rooms. If it were not so, would I have told you that I go to prepare a place for you? And if I go and prepare a place for you, I will come again and will take you to myself, that where I am you may be also. (John 14:1–3)

John was the only disciple to record these words. Maybe that's the reason he is the only one who got to visit heaven and get a glimpse of our future.

> After this I looked, and behold, a door standing open in heaven! And the first

voice, which I had heard speaking to me like a trumpet, said, "Come up here, and I will show you what must take place after this." At once I was in the Spirit, and behold, a throne stood in heaven, with one seated on the throne. (Revelation 4:1–2)

While you and I probably won't travel to heaven as John did, that doesn't mean that we can't experience something similar.

But, as it is written,

"What no eye has seen, nor ear heard, nor the heart of man imagined, what God has prepared for those who love him"— these things God has revealed to us through the Spirit. For the Spirit searches everything, even the depths of God. (1 Corinthians 2:9–10)

This speaks of a mysterious and miraculous experience that is available to you. In fact, Paul expects this for all believers. We can experience something without seeing, hearing, or imagining. Don't overanalyze this, just believe it. Just expect and enjoy it. Ask the Holy Spirit to reveal "what God has prepared for those who love him." Have faith that God is more than capable of revealing things to you without using your eyes and ears. Expect your loving Father to minister to your soul in a way that you'll find yourself longing for a place you've never been to be with your Beloved whom you've never seen.

Lisa and I regularly visited her grandma Clara during her final year on earth. She was ninety-one and had lived a life filled with suffering, but her trials only brought her closer to Jesus. She remains one of the sweetest people I have ever met. In hindsight, I wish we had spent more time with her when we had the chance. During one of our last visits, she told us about how she would go to bed with excitement each night. She would pray and ask, "Lord, is tonight the night that I get to see You? I can't wait to see You!" There was absolutely no fear or doubt in her. She had only confidence and anticipation in her eyes. Even as I write this and recall her countenance, I'm telling God that I want my life to end in the same way. That level of supernatural peace came from years of sweet fellowship with Jesus. She had fought the good fight. She had kept the faith. Her love endured to the end.

That's what I want for all of you. Not just to make it through this life hanging on by your fingernails but to finish with joy, anticipation, excitement for eternity, and an unshakable confidence in the love of God.

Throughout this book, we've been exploring what it means to be the beloved of God. We've seen that this isn't just a nice title—it's our deepest identity, purchased at the highest price. We've uncovered the lies that keep us from living in this truth, and we've discovered the practices that help us abide in His love. Now, as we come to the end, I want to remind you of the simplest and most profound truth: you are loved by God. Not for what you do. Not because you've earned it. But because He chose to set His affection on you before the foundation of the world.

This love is not fleeting or conditional. It's not based on your performance or dependent on your perfection. It's as eternal and unchanging as God Himself. When your love grows cold, His remains constant. When you feel alone, He is still with you. When the enemy attacks, God fights for you.

My prayer for you, beloved, is not that your life would be easy but that it would be anchored. Anchored in the love of the Father who gave His Son for you. Anchored in the grace of Jesus who died and rose again for you. Anchored in the power of the Spirit who lives and works in you.

Be loved, beloved. Not just today, but forever.

I can think of no better way to end this book than to print the last two chapters of the Bible. Take your time and meditate on each phrase of this passage. Ask the Spirit to mysteriously reveal the wonders of this passage to your soul. Come, Holy Spirit. Show your beloved what you have prepared for us.

REVELATION

Chapter Twenty-One

¹Then I saw a new heaven and a new earth, for the first heaven and the first earth had passed away, and the sea was no more. ²And I saw the holy city, new Jerusalem, coming down out of heaven from God, prepared as a bride adorned for her husband. ³And I heard a loud voice from the throne saying, "Behold, the dwelling place of God is with man. He will dwell with them, and they will be his people, and God himself will be with them as their God. ⁴He will wipe away every tear from their eyes, and death shall be no more, neither shall there be mourning, nor crying, nor pain anymore, for the former things have passed away."

⁵And he who was seated on the throne said, "Behold, I am making all things new." Also he said, "Write this down, for these words are trustworthy and true." ⁶And he said to me, "It is done! I am the Alpha and the Omega, the beginning and the end. To the thirsty I will give from the spring of the water of life without payment. ⁷The one who conquers will have this heritage, and I will be his God and he will be my son. ⁸But as for the cowardly, the faithless, the detestable, as for murderers, the sexually immoral, sorcerers, idolaters, and all liars, their portion will be in the lake that burns with fire and sulfur, which is the second death."

The New Jerusalem

⁹Then came one of the seven angels who had the seven bowls full of the seven last plagues and spoke to me, saying, "Come, I will show you the Bride, the wife of the Lamb." ¹⁰And he carried me away in the Spirit to a great, high mountain, and showed me the holy city Jerusalem coming down out of heaven from God, ¹¹having the glory of God, its radiance like a most rare jewel, like a jasper, clear as crystal. ¹²It had a

great, high wall, with twelve gates, and at the gates twelve angels, and on the gates the names of the twelve tribes of the sons of Israel were inscribed—[13]on the east three gates, on the north three gates, on the south three gates, and on the west three gates. [14]And the wall of the city had twelve foundations, and on them were the twelve names of the twelve apostles of the Lamb.

[15]And the one who spoke with me had a measuring rod of gold to measure the city and its gates and walls. [16]The city lies foursquare, its length the same as its width. And he measured the city with his rod, 12,000 stadia. Its length and width and height are equal. [17]He also measured its wall, 144 cubits by human measurement, which is also an angel's measurement. [18]The wall was built of jasper, while the city was pure gold, like clear glass. [19]The foundations of the wall of the city were adorned with every kind of jewel. The first was jasper, the second sapphire, the third agate, the fourth emerald, [20]the fifth onyx, the sixth carnelian, the seventh chrysolite, the eighth beryl, the ninth topaz, the tenth chrysoprase, the eleventh jacinth, the twelfth amethyst. [21]And the twelve gates were twelve pearls, each of the gates made of a single pearl, and the street of the city was pure gold, like transparent glass.

[22]And I saw no temple in the city, for its temple is the Lord God the Almighty and the Lamb. [23]And the city has no need of sun or moon to shine on it, for the glory of God gives it light, and its lamp is the Lamb. [24]By its light will the nations walk, and the kings of the earth will bring their glory into it, [25]and its gates will never be shut by day—and there will be no night there. [26]They will bring into it the glory and the honor of the nations. [27]But nothing unclean will ever enter it, nor anyone who does what is detestable or false, but only those who are written in the Lamb's book of life.

REVELATION

Chapter Twenty-Two

¹Then the angel showed me the river of the water of life, bright as crystal, flowing from the throne of God and of the Lamb ²through the middle of the street of the city; also, on either side of the river, the tree of life with its twelve kinds of fruit, yielding its fruit each month. The leaves of the tree were for the healing of the nations. ³No longer will there be anything accursed, but the throne of God and of the Lamb will be in it, and his servants will worship him. ⁴They will see his face, and his name will be on their foreheads. ⁵And night will be no more. They will need no light of lamp or sun, for the Lord God will be their light, and they will reign forever and ever.

Jesus is Coming

⁶And he said to me, "These words are trustworthy and true. And the Lord, the God of the spirits of the prophets, has sent his angel to show his servants what must soon take place." ⁷"And behold, I am coming soon. Blessed is the one who keeps the words of the prophecy of this book." ⁸I, John, am the one who heard and saw these things. And when I heard and saw them, I fell down to worship at the feet of the angel who showed them to me, ⁹but he said to me, "You must not do that! I am a fellow servant with you and your brothers the prophets, and with those who keep the words of this book. Worship God." ¹⁰And he said to me, "Do not seal up the words of the prophecy of this book, for the time is near. ¹¹Let the evildoer still do evil, and the filthy still be filthy, and the righteous still do right, and the holy still be holy." ¹²"Behold, I am coming soon, bringing my recompense with me, to repay each one for what he has done. ¹³I am the Alpha and the Omega, the first and the last, the beginning and the end." ¹⁴Blessed are those who wash their robes, so that they may have the right to the

tree of life and that they may enter the city by the gates. ¹⁵Outside are the dogs and sorcerers and the sexually immoral and murderers and idolaters, and everyone who loves and practices falsehood. ¹⁶"I, Jesus, have sent my angel to testify to you about these things for the churches. I am the root and the descendant of David, the bright morning star." ¹⁷The Spirit and the Bride say, "Come." And let the one who hears say, "Come." And let the one who is thirsty come; let the one who desires take the water of life without price. ¹⁸I warn everyone who hears the words of the prophecy of this book: if anyone adds to them, God will add to him the plagues described in this book, ¹⁹and if anyone takes away from the words of the book of this prophecy, God will take away his share in the tree of life and in the holy city, which are described in this book. ²⁰He who testifies to these things says, "Surely I am coming soon." Amen. Come, Lord Jesus! ²¹The grace of the Lord Jesus be with all. Amen.